LAND OF
SACRED LEGENDS

I wish to thank Eve Goldsmith for all her artwork and the Rev Brenda Catherall for her help throughout the research.

Candida Boyes gave me vauable advice on the visual merit of the sites and made many useful suggestions for revisions of the manuscript.

Graham Murphy

LAND OF
SACRED LEGENDS

A Guide to
Early Christian Sites in North West Wales

Graham Murphy

Illustrations by Eve Goldsmith

Published by Sigma Leisure – an imprint of
Sigma Press, Stobart House, Pontyclerc, Penybanc Road, Ammanford, Carmarthenshire SA18 3HP.

British Library Cataloguing in Publication Data
A CIP record for this book is available from the British Library.

ISBN: 978-1-85058-931-0

Typesetting and Design by: Sigma Press, Ammanford.

Cover picture: Ffynnon Seiriol, Penmon © Eve Goldsmith

Pictures: © Eve Goldsmith

Printed by: TJ International Ltd, Padstow, Cornwall

Why so fast,
mortal? These very seas
are baptised. The parish
has a saint's name time cannot
unfrock. In cities that
have outgrown their promise people
are becoming pilgrims again.

RS Thomas, *The Moon in Lleyn*

YNYS MÔN
ANGLESEY

PENMON →

LLANGADWALADR +

YNYS LLANDDWYN +

ARFON

CLYNNOG FAWR +

LLANAELHAEARN +
PISTYLL +

LLANGYBI +

LLANNOR +

LLANGWNNADL +

LLŶN

ABERDARON +

+ YNYS ENLLI
BARDSEY ISLAND

CONTENTS

Coastal Map 6

Introduction 9

Chapter 1   Dwynwen in Love – Llanddwyn 15

Chapter 2   A King Lampooned – Llangadwaladr 21

Chapter 3   Pale Seiriol – Penmon 29

Chapter 4   Beuno, Restorer of the unjustly slain 35
             – Clynnog Fawr and Llanaelhaearn

Chapter 5   Cybi's Well – Llangybi 45

Chapter 6   Figulinus's plea to a heavenly mathematician ... 55
             – Llannor

Chapter 7   The Pilgrim Path – Pistyll and Llangwnnadl ... 63

Chapter 8   Senacus caught in a net – Bardsey Island ... 73
             and Aberdaron

Conclusion 83

Ordnance Survey Site Location References 85

Opening Times of Churches 87

Post-Roman Latin Inscribed Stones – Anglesey and ... 89
   the Llŷn Peninsula

Sacred Wells and their Churches – Anglesey and the Llŷn ... 95
   Peninsula

Conservation 105

Bibliography 107

Tea Shops 111

Ffynnon Seiriol, Penmon

INTRODUCTION

The pilgrimage routes to Bardsey Island are followed by walkers along the Llŷn coastal paths. My concern has been to chart a less direct course through Gwynedd (Latin name *Veneda*) visiting a few more of the early Christian sites. These are already mentioned in various guide books, but I was aware that there was scope for a different approach, one which recognised the importance of the legends and a more in-depth interpretation of the Latin inscriptions. Having set about the task, I found myself corresponding with historians and archaeologists and reading 'lives' of the saints; the result of this work is, I hope, of interest to anyone for whom the history of the early Welsh kingdoms is unfamiliar territory.

It needs to be borne in mind that there is no authorised version of what I describe as the sacred legends; these vary according to the approach taken by scribes and poets; my own re-telling is set down in italics to give them an identity next to other information from stories of the saints. The legends were devised to attract pilgrims to a shrine or a holy well where miracles occurred.

These fascinating locations are described in the chapters and are fairly accessible despite minor obstacles such as steps, stiles and irregular footpaths.

The sacred legends are events set in a time-frame between AD400 and AD650; two centuries and more of insecure history that followed the departure of the Roman legions. As Saxon warlords seized the south-east of Britain and suppressed the Roman lifestyle with its literacy and learning, to preserve their religion some Christian communities sought safety in the west. They resettled in a more rugged terrain of mountains and coastlands where languages and culture connected them closely with Celtic Ireland, Scotland, the Isle of Man, Cornwall and Brittany. Christianity in Gwynedd would have begun with the Romans, but this influx of refugees would seem partly to account for the archaeological evidence in the years that followed.

It is a cause for confusion that the post-Roman period can be variously described as sub-Roman, the Dark Ages, the Heroic Age and the Age of Saints. The last of these titles is not inconsistent with the signs of Christianity around the Celtic sea. Some of the saints were wandering monks, living in isolation or in the company of 'bretheren'. They sailed the seaways to establish churches and monasteries close to the shoreline or in the shelter of estuaries. The great majority of the saints in Wales, however, were not wanderers but settled and many lived in families; their degree of spirituality ranged from a life devoted to prayer – some of the men were priests and bishops – to being nominally Christian.

Ffynnon Ddwynwen, Llanddwyn

Almost half of the Welsh saints are known only by the dedication of a single church. This rather implies that their sanctity was conferred because of their presentation of land for use as a cemetery (the average size is 0.31 hectare) and as a place for regular worship.

The first churches erected in such consecrated grounds would normally be small and built of wood rather than stone. The word *llan*, usually translated as 'church', originally described an enclosed plot of 'land'. Hence, we have *perllan* as Welsh for an 'orchard' and *corlan* for a 'sheepfold'; but rather than a prefix the saint's name is a suffix. In the parish church at Llansadwrn, which is mainly Victorian, there is a sixth century epitaph stone inscribed to Saturninus, Latinised Sadwrn. He was the patron saint to whom the first church was dedicated.

Whatever the original boundary, what we see today enclosing these burial grounds is usually a stone wall, except where the *llan* is a very small island with the sea for protection. Sometimes this wall circles the site, emphasising the fact that the *llan* is much earlier than the fields which divide the land into squares and rectangles.

In idyllic rural scenery it is easy to weave fantasies about 'Celtic Christianity', but despite a different calendar and a distinctive monasticism, the Christianty of the Celts did not break from Rome. Yet the myth persists. When set amid trees, the little low church can look as if it is rooted in a druidic grove. Indeed some of the yew trees can be very ancient. Close by is the well (*ffynnon*) possibly perceived as a doorway to the underworld even after it was dedicated in the name of the saint. Archaeological excavation confirms that some wells are pre-Christian and some, of course, are still visited for purposes of healing; a more sinister fact is that a few of the wells were depositories for curses written with malice on pieces of slate. Terrified at the prospect of a pagan revival, in AD567 a Christian Council meeting at Tours condemned rituals everywhere beside springs, rocks and trees. This was excessive. Nearly all of the *llannau* have some association with these wonders of nature about which there are often quite innocent traditions. The papacy proved to be far more pragmatic, encouraging the appropriation of pre-Christian holy sites provided they were cleansed of their heathen past. Clusters of trees, sacred *ffynhonnau*, mysterious boulders, all add to the fascination of a Welsh country church.

Newborough Forest

CHAPTER 1

DWYNWEN IN LOVE

LLANDDWYN

Llanddwyn Island lies off one of the most beautiful beaches in Gwynedd, a long ribbon of sand replenished from tides that run across Caernarfon Bay and into the Menai Strait. Its historical significance derives from the post-Roman period, when the territory that is now Wales was at least seven separate kingdoms. The way to this hallowed ground lies along the tracks that pass through Newborough Forest, one of which starts as a lane running south-west from the village of Newborough and beside the foundations of a medieval villa (*llys*). A settlement (*maerdref*) called Rhosyr extended from this spacious dwelling on land which in Roman times had been cleared of a primeval oakwood for cultivation and grazing.

Patronised by the kings of Gwynedd, Rhosyr was prosperous throughout the Middle Ages. Its fortunes declined when the surrounding fields became inundated with sand, the result of a change in the prevailing climate. By the end of the sixteenth century this *maerdref* was abandoned, smothered by the dunes. It was finally buried in the 1940s, courtesy of the Forestry Commission with Corsican pine; instead of Rhosyr's inhabitants there are now colonies of red squirrels and ink black ravens tumbling on the winds. At the westerly edge of the densely planted pines, the spine of Llanddwyn stretches south-west into the oncoming sea; treeless and sandy, covered in marram grass, heather, burnet rose and a countless variety of wind blown small flowers tolerant of the brine.

This beautiful island with its disused lighthouse and a single row of cottages is cut off only when the sea is exceptionally high; it is nearly always accessible and draws the explorer in all moods and weather. Small coves cradle the tides as they come in from the south, whilst at the northern edge low cliffs cause the incoming waves to shatter and roar. The rock pools here are raggedly laced with thrift and samphire, bright pink and yellow against the blackened seaweed. Forlorn at the centre of this airy wilderness are the remains of a church (p104), built at the height of a devotion to St Dwynwen, for whom this *llan* was both a hermitage and a garden.

Almost in living memory, a parody of Dwynwen's cult was a somewhat comical feature of the dunes nearest to the island. An elderly woman played the role of a fortune-teller, predicting to summer visitors (in exchange for a small fee) the geographical location of their future partners. Such privileged information was divined by the study of a few small fish, as they swam in the compass of Crochan Llanddwyn, a pool now silted and drained dry by the woods. That Dwynwen's legend is much about celibacy seems not to have been understood by her eager audience, primed as it was for good luck and good fortune:

Maelon and Dwynwen fell deeply in love. However, Dwynwen refused marriage and in anger Maelon left her. She then prayed to be cured of her inordinate desire. The Lord of Heaven heard her entreaties and offered her a chalice from which she eagerly drank, whence all her deep longings for Maelon subsided. But the chalice was then passed to the luckless Maelon. As he quaffed from the cup he suddenly turned to ice. In horror for this occurrence, Dwynwen renewed her prayers, earnestly and fervently, and again the heaven's Lord was moved to grant her, not one, but three powerful wishes. With the first she warmed Maelon and restored him to life. With the second she decreed that all true lovers who entered a plea with her should either succeed or be cured of their passion. Her final wish was never to marry.

As a mediatrix of erotic love, Dwynwen's ability to summon the Almighty came to be respected not simply because she had been a convert to Christianity but also because she was empowered magically, or so it seemed, as a pagan priestess; unquestionably of Celtic stock, she appears in genealogy as one of the twenty-four, beautiful and virtuous daughters of Brychan; fifth century ruler of the kingdom of Brycheiniog. Her feast day, 25 January, is still celebrated in Wales as if she were a St Valentine, determined to unite lovers wherever they may be.

Typically for a minor saint, Dwynwen was also revered locally throughout the Middle Ages as a healer of all that lives. In addition to drinking from the spring (*ffynnon* – see p11) that was her well, either to cure love or to arouse love in another, there were sufferers from bone diseases who spent nights sleeping on the rock known as Gwely Esyth, 'Bed of the Bier', reputed to be the site of Dwynwen's island tomb. Sadly, this landmark can no longer be seen. A saint's earthly remains were thought to radiate healing in much the same manner as embers shed their heat; the practice of lying on top of the grave was known as 'sacred incubation'. To extend this aspect of her veneration, yet further restorative powers were sought of St Dwynwen to bring order to the world through intercessory prayer; candles were lit in the entrance to her shrine for the well being and safety of all manner of livestock.

By the middle of the seventeenth century, cultic practices at Llanddwyn had been abandoned in keeping with the more rational spirit of the post-Reformation age. Respect for the saint had all but disappeared until a farmer at Bodowen, working in sight of the island from the north, innocently put his oxen to the plough on 25 April, the Feast of St Mark. This had once been a day devoted to prayer. His normally docile beasts went completely mad, ran over a cliff, plunged into the sea and instantly drowned. Horrified, the parishioners at nearby Llangadwaladr paid for the repair of the dilapidated church porch where they resumed their payers and their votive candles in the hope of averting any future catastrophe. This return to despised superstition so enraged Protestant Christians that they in turn set about wrecking what remained of the holy wells. The island was a hive of sectarian activity, to the delight of sceptics and scornful atheists. By 1906, there was enough of the church standing for the architect of Portmeirion, Clough Williams-Ellis, to propose its restoration. But his desire to reroof the building fell on deaf ears.

The very high regard in which Dwynwen was once held can be seen in some lines written by the poet Dafydd ap Gwilym. In the fourteenth century, he stood by candlelight beneath a statue of the saint, one of the many pilgrims anxious for blessings. He pleaded his longing for Morfudd, the one whom he loved, and in the shadows felt a sense of deep consolation that no-one could depart from sanctuary of this island burdened 'with sickness or a heavy mind'. Fixing his gaze on the likeness of Dwynwen, all covered in gold, she was as the 'beauty of tears of hoar-frost' (*deigr arien degwch*).

For all the strangeness of Dwynwen's sacred legend, it retains a hold on the imaginations of many who hear of it. The story gives to this extraordinary saint a unique identity as a Celtic heroine of the life of prayer – living, as far as we shall ever know, in monastic simplicity and unshakeable faith. The beauty of her *llan* also plays a part. On a still summer's evening the island and the sea, close by the forest, are a world of lost voices, secretly expressed longings, subtle and sweet fragrances and colours softening to the onset of the night.

Llangadwaldr East Window, detail

CHAPTER 2

A KING LAMPOONED

LLANGADWALADR

Four miles north-west of Newborough Forest, beyond the Malltraeth Sands, lies the village of Aberffraw. There is nothing now to indicate its importance in the Middle Ages when, on the gentle rise above the river, there was, from the fifth to the thirteen centuries, the seat of Venedotian kings. A picturesque old bridge with an elliptical arch spans the slow meander of Afon Ffraw, while from the top of the village a lane runs west to the sea and a little church set on the islet of St Cwyfan, a sixth century preacher whose mission was to Ireland. Beside the lane and at the edge of the village there is another small church, dedicated to St Beuno. Rebuilt in the Tudor period, it has a Romanesque arch with bestial heads. Connected with Aberffraw there is another place of worship two miles inland along the road to Newborough as it runs due east. Llangadwaldr, it has to be said, is exceptionally well hidden, behind a stuccoed vicarage of late Georgian provenance and a magnificent stand of chestnut trees.

A three-bell turret and an impressive gothic window (p86) are among the outward signs of architectural adornment that are a little surprising when attached to a nave of the thirteenth century in such a rural location. The first church on this site was founded six centuries earlier, sometime around AD650, by Cadwaladr, a king of Gwynedd who saw himself as particularly saintly and of a family he wished to portray as devoutly Christian. From a modern perspective he evidently succeeded by being notably less war-like than his belligerent ancestors. Although his detractors criticised him as a 'battle-shunner', Cadwaldr achieved beatification and was hailed by Pope Sergius as a model of Christian kingship. The disestablishment of the Church of England in Wales in the twentieth century caused Llangadwaldr a near catastrophic decline in income and extensive disrepair. Threatened with disuse, this building was only narrowly saved for the continuance of worship in 2004, by the fundraising efforts of a handful of parishioners.

The scale of the heritage can be seen on entering. Two wealthy Anglesey families were responsible for the chapels; the Meyricks of Bodorgan paid for the north chapel and its Victorian stained glass, whilst the south chapel with its fine Jacobean memorial was a gift of the Owens of Bodowen. The medieval east window is one of the few in Wales to have survived the Reformation, largely intact, during which time it was dismantled and kept hidden in a vault. Commissioned by Meurig ap Llywellyn and his wife, Marged, the three lights of stained glass would seem to be in gratitude for the safe return of their son Owain from the Battle of Bosworth in 1485. The family is portrayed in the lower half; Owain kneels in battle dress emblazoned with three ravens, the Celtic symbol for success in war, while Erin his wife follows him in an attitude of prayer. Cadwaladr sits in parliament robes as if he were contemporary. In the central panel between the Virgin Mary and St John there is an astonishing depiction of Christ crucified; eyes downcast and his body drained of blood caught by the angels, his bones show up as if under an x-ray as a reminder of life's transience amid the scenes of earthly power.

There is one feature in the whole of this building which can be identified for certain as having come from the earlier church. It is an inscribed rectangular stone set in the north wall of the nave. Ornate lettering makes the Latin appear difficult to decipher, but what we are looking at is the work of a genius, one who in the mid seventh century dared to create a subversive commentary within the shape of a pious text. In 2002, Professor Charles Thomas succeeded in demonstrating that the design of this inscription cleverly perpetuates a deep sense of bitterness that had been poisoning the atmosphere hereabout through several generations, setting the church against the royal household.

To understand this dispute we need to refer to the first history of Britain, written by a brilliant and impetuous monk by the name of Gildas. He lived long and industriously throughout most of the sixth century. His *De Excidio Britanniae*, 'On the Ruin of Britain', condemned British kings in general and did not spare the House of Gwynedd. Gildas accused his contemporary, King Maelgwn, of having murdered both his queen and his nephew in order to gain the hand in marriage of his nephew's widow. Rather than weaken over time, distaste for the morals of Venedotian royalty seems to have become entrenched as Gildas's diatribe circulated and found a ready audience in the British monasteries. Some hundred years after its publication, King Cadwaladr was desperate to repair this damage. To reinstate the reputation of his dynasty he might have preferred to commemorate his father, Cadwallon, who in an alliance with Penda of Mercia had attacked the Northumbrians and killed the English king Edwin. But subsequently Cadwallon had been slaughtered in battle, by Edwin's successor Oswald, in AD 634. At that time his body was lost to the enemy and could not be commemorated with a monumental tomb. However, Cadwaladr's grandfather Cadfan's reputation had also been blighted by the greed and immorality that had been so effectively attached to the name of Maelgwn; more so for being a generation closer to the arch offender. With the building of a new church, Cadwaladr was determined, once and for all, with help from those whose hero had maligned him, to rewrite in glory his family history.

The installation of a eulogy to Cadfan was, to put it mildly, unappealing to the clergy, but the orders of the king required their obedience. Only when a decision was taken for the inscription to be carved in a fashionable 'book hand' and not in Roman capitals, did the churchmen realise this project was wide open to sabotage. Letters of the proposed style are florid, not rigid, and just as in an illuminated manuscript, they lend themselves to a cartoon-like imagery (cf the beginnings of pictorial elements in the *Cathach* psalter and culminating around AD800 in the *Book of Kells*).

After his death, Cadfan's body was probably entombed at Aberffraw. At the consecration of the new church it would then have been taken to Llangadwaladr and re-interred close to the altar. Centuries later, these royal

King Cadfan Stone
CATAMANUS REX SAPIENTISIMUS OPINATISIMUS OMNIUM REGUM
'*Cadfan, king, wisest, most-renowned of-all kings*'

remains were disturbed yet again, when the church was rebuilt and also when it was enlarged. There are in all likelihood no longer any relics behind the stone, but the inscription is as clear as on the day it was carved and no doubt read aloud to a delighted King Cadwaladr. To the modern reader the letters appear hopelessly outlandish, but they are easily deciphered, bearing in mind that what looks like r is actually s, and that the *a* letters are somewhat peculiar.

To appreciate the inscription as a revival of Gildas's attack, the reader needs to bear in mind how early medieval manuscripts sometimes incorporate the figurative shapes of men and beasts. The letters carved in the stone appear in places inexplicably exaggerated, but by their size, angle and juxtaposition, they hint at certain body parts. The letters *o* align like a pair of eyes (*oculi*) and the enlarged letters *a* can conceivably be taken for the ears (*aures*) of a beast. The animal in reference becomes clear when it is realised that there is a spelling variation in the Latin word for 'most renowned'; *opinatisimus*, should ideally have ss in the middle, but would not then be an anagram for *optimus asini*, 'the best of an ass'. According to the well known proverb the best of an ass is undoubtedly its ears. A thought is implanted of Cadfan's affinity with the legendary Midas, ass-eared Greek king who foolishly wished that everything he touched would be turned into gold.

Not content with one satirical jibe there is seemingly another; a cynic might abstract the letters from lines three and four. *Ornatus*, meaning 'embellishment', is as much a double entendre in Latin as in English, but a euphemism is hardly required when the correct word is spelt out in five of the eight letters toward the end of line two. A well educated reader, furthermore, would not have failed to wonder at the enlarged word for 'king'. The incompetent stonemason should surely have been dismissed before an extra limb on the *x*, for *rex*, had produced a rude stick man in amorous conjunction with a cringing letter *e*. Or was it rather that he was carefully supervised? The waggling limb of the letter *r* tends not to allay suspicion and for readers of the Bible there is yet something else. The epithet 'wisest' attributes to Cadfan the wisdom of Solomon and, unavoidably, the flaw in the king's character, namely his improprieties with foreign women (*I Kings* 11.1-6). Overtly Cadfan is here commemorated as heroic and discrete, but the subtext tells us that he was a degenerate philanderer, or to put it another way, a 'sex-crazed ass'. With this monument, far from being undermined, Gildas's view of the family is reinforced!

That the inscription was not defaced shows that the clergy were able to state their case without ever arousing the suspicion of Cadwaladr or his successors, however often the royals must have come to the church and wondered at its artistry. At the heart of Gwynedd a feisty Christianity was alive and well. Not all of Britain was in the 'Dark Ages'. Clerics of the Celtic Church were capable of demonstrating their true feelings, surreptitiously, even when under orders to fabricate an inscription they regarded as a lie.

Penmon Priory

CHAPTER 3

PALE SEIRIOL

PENMON

The route to Penmon from the south-west of Anglesey and the Menai bridges is via the main road through the centre of Beaumaris. This skirts the castle, follows the shoreline and then turns due north toward Llangoed. Before the village, a sign to Penmon, off to the right, indicates a country lane that winds like a serpent and eventually runs along the top of a sea dyke in the general direction of Penmon Point. Ahead is a low hill with limestone quarries and the half ruined buildings of an Augustinian priory.

The original foundation on this site was a *clas* monastery on land which had been given early in the sixth century by the Venedotian King Einion to his kinsman Seiriol. There were similar religious communities at Bangor, Caergybi, Llaneilian, Clynnog Fawr, Beddgelert and Aberdaron. A *clas* was a 'mother church', usually administered by the heirs of a single family. Its monks and clergy were sometimes married. They and their wives committed themselves to a life of prayer and, in addition, they undertook pastoral work for 'daughter churches' supported by tithes of agricultural produce. This spiritual welfare system was highly successful and operated throughout

Wales until the Normans superseded the *clasau* with continental religious orders. At Penmon, the later Augustinian Rule entailed what had become, by the thirteenth century, an entirely celibate order of monks.

A flight of steps ascends from the road and into the prior's courtyard. From here there is a door to the Victorian chancel of what is, for the most part, a twelfth century church. St Seiriol's has survived considerable restoration with Romanesque features lovingly preserved. Inside, beneath the crossing tower, the west arch is just one example of the perfection of detail; re-set in the south transept there are two rows of colonettes, handsomely carved with cushioned capitols and chevrons. Also here, letting in light through the transept east wall, there is a small stained glass depiction of St Seiriol and St Chistopher carrying the Christ child above an incoming tide. This was once part of the medieval east window when the saint of travellers was an object of contemplation for any one intending to walk across the sands, a route to the mainland then commonly in use but potentially treacherous. The two large stone crosses are from around AD1000 and were brought in from where they once stood at the immediate boundary of monastic land. The wheelcross was desecrated when put to use as a lintel and ground flat entirely along the length of one edge; it is still very beautiful. With their Scandinavian frets (located in the transept) interlace and Manx ring chain (located in the nave) these pillars of Celtic art are a pure delight. Half way down the nave cross and barely visible, there is a figure of Anthony, saint of the Egyptian desert, in torment from demons whispering in his ears. He was a model of the hermit life who was much admired by the Celtic monks.

Above an ancient south door on the outside of the nave, the figure of a dragon is cleverly adapted to creep across the tympanum of a single stone, biting its tail. The Prior's house next to the church is privately occupied and on the south side of the courtyard there is the shell of a three storey building wrecked at the Reformation. This was cellar, refectory and dormitory before its roof was stripped, the usual way of ensuring that a monastery was no longer viable. In contrast to this ruin, a few yards to the east stands a seventeenth century dovecot in robust condition, built in the style of the French Renaissance.

To one side of the monks' fish pond a path rises gently away from the road and enters a small enclosure. Here the imagination can take wing and transport the visitor further back in time. A circle of stones, thought to be those on the site of Seiriol's cell, lies close to a restored well house, St Seiriol's Well, a source of water for baptisms and healing (see p8).

Of the several hundred holy wells in Wales a sizeable number have been lost to land improvement. Seiriol's has survived. Imperceptibly, the spring, this *ffynnon*, still rises from somewhere deep in the carboniferous rock. Even a hardened sceptic would concede that this scene is one which evokes a sense of timeless tranquillity. Thirteen miles north-west there were once two holy wells at the place called Clorach, but a road has been built which has effectively destroyed them. Named after Seiriol and the Celtic monk Cybi, these are now covered over and almost nothing remains. Fortunately, St Cybi is better commemorated on the Llŷn peninsula and elsewhere on Anglesey, notably at Caergybi (Holyhead) where the walls and towers of the Roman fort (caer) given him by the otherwise maligned King Maelgwn make a rather grand courtyard for the parish church. But it was at Clorach, according to legend, that the two monks used to meet:

From Penmon in the east, Seiriol walked with his back to the sun and likewise on his return. Thus was his complexion made pale and he was known as Seiriol Wyn (white). Cybi from his monastery in the west faced the sun even as he set out, and likewise on his return. He is Cybi Felyn (tawny).

This story has inspired representations in Christian art at various locations throughout North Wales. The best known is on a richly painted icon in the Orthodox church at Blaenau Ffestiniog where it is not Clorach that appears but the well house at Penmon – a bright blue ribbon of water irrigates a land of gilded mountains blessed with the feet of the two peaceful saints. Not to be out done, in the chancel at Penmon there is a modern stained glass window showing the saints with different complexions beneath a depiction of 'Christ stilling the Storm', yet another reminder of the perilous sea.

The road to Penmon Priory does not end there but continues beyond a toll gate, over a rugged wetland full of meadowsweet and marsh orchid, past a cottage café and its garden and on to the shore and the sea at Trwyn Du. Off the coast is Ynys Seiriol, a wildlife reserve known by the English as Puffin Island. At its centre there are the remains of an oval enclosure, cells, a cloister and a somewhat bleak church tower. This isolated spot was useful for retreats and eventually became a separate monastery. In 1188, the medieval topographer, Gerald of Wales, found Ynys Seiriol to be occupied by monks who were living 'from manual labour and serving God' (*Itinerarium Cambriae*). Today these ruins are an untroubled sanctuary for guillemot, shag, razorbill, kittiwake and the wonderfully dark and heraldic-looking cormorant.

St Beuno's Church, Clynnog Fawr

CHAPTER 4

BEUNO, RESTORER OF THE UNJUSTLY SLAIN

CLYNNOG FAWR AND LLANAELHAEARN

Having reached the most easterly point of the legend-trail, we leave Penmon and journey south-west, having crossed the Menai Strait. Beyond Caernarfon and west of Llanwnda is Clynnog Fawr (sometimes known as Llanfeuno) and a large, embattled late medieval church built on the site of a monastery founded by St Beuno in the seventh century. Stories of his life are to be found in the *Buchedd Beuno*, written in 1346 by an anchorite of Llanddewibrefi in Ceredigion. Much of what follows is derived from that source.

Born of a noble family near Wroxeter (east of Shrewsbury) the future saint was tutored by the monks of Caerwent and subsequently established a monastery at Berriew, twenty-five miles to the west. His circumstances can be compared to those of the Dalai Lama who felt driven into exile. Walking beside the River Severn one day, Beuno was seized with a deep sense of foreboding when he heard from the opposite bank a Saxon warrior training dogs to chase a hare. The warlike bellowing seemed to affirm what he had always feared, that under these invaders there would never be a real peace;

hence the resolution to leave his homeland. Before setting out, Beuno pressed an acorn into the ground above his father's grave. From this seed there grew an oak so large that it was wryly rumoured to be fatal to the English who passed beneath its bough. Crossing the Berwyn Hills, the fugitive stayed awhile at Gwyddelwern and from here he went north-east to what is now called Holywell, to establish a church and to tutor his niece, Winefride, before turning west in the direction of Gwynedd. On reaching the court of Cadwallon, Beuno bargained a rod of gold in exchange for land near to the dwelling of his cousin Baglan, saint of Llanfaglan. But unbeknown to him this pasture was not the king's property. While building the *llan* wall, he heard the plaintiff cry of a fractious infant and in conversation with its mother was soon made aware that the land he had paid for was an inheritance of the child. Overcome with fury, Beuno put a curse on Cadwallon and was only pacified when the king's cousin, Gwyddaint, offered him Clynnog Fawr (Great Holly Grove) as compensation. Here, in AD616, a monastery was established amid rumours of miracles: a turtle dove in Llwyn Nef (Heavenly Grove) entranced the monks with its cooing; Beuno had only to pray and the bird would disappear. Crossing a rough sea to preach on Llanddwyn, Beuno's precious manuscript was blown away by the wind; a curlew swooped down, plucked it from the swell and used its long beak to set it down at his landing. It appeared that the abbot had druidic-like powers.

Since its diversion in 2009, the A499 to Pwllheli sweeps past Clynnog Fawr leaving St Beuno's Church cut off from the sea. Built around 1500, this stranded ark was meant to accommodate great assemblies of pilgrims on their northern route to the Island of Bardsey. The interior is airy, full of bouncing light from hundreds of clear glass panes; the walls are lime washed, the floor is lime stone flagged and the magnificent roof is held aloft with main beams resting alternately on wall-posts and hammer-beams. But what should have been a space perpetually resounding to the intonation of psalms and prayers is now eerily silent, and so generally spartan that the eye craves for fine details. The choir stalls are one of the places where there is beauty to be discovered: poppy-heads, vine leaves, heads of the clergy, eagles and panels of linen fold, all finely carved. Cyff Beuno, the offerings chest, by way of contrast, was crudely fashioned from a single tree trunk in a time when the imperfections of all sentient beings could be attoned with 'guilt money'. Herds of cattle were systematically culled by superstitious farmers hoping to gain favour with God and the Church; calves and lambs born with a deformity were said to have Nôd Beuno, the 'Mark of Beuno'. On Trinity Sundays these lesser beasts were driven into the burial yard and sold to defray the expenses of clergy and building; money from these sales accumulated in the *cyff*.

Beneath the church tower there is an entrance to a corridor, usually kept locked. This leads to a sixteenth century Capel y Bedd, a chapel above the place where the saint was laid to rest. Beuno's death occurred sometime in the middle of the seventh century and all that remains here from early monasticism is an eighth century stone (Maen Beuno) incised with a cross. But outside in the burial ground, close by the chapel, there is a tall granite sundial from the tenth or eleventh century. A divided semi-circle at the top of this pillar shows the intervals for work between the times of prayer.

Going a little way along the village road in a westerly direction there is a holy well, Ffynnon Beuno; a roofless chamber with seats around it and steps to the pool. The sick would be immersed here before sleeping overnight in Beuno's Chapel, laid on a bed of rushes on the floor above the place that was said to be his grave. This well water was thought to be especially effective as a medicine for epilepsy and, when mixed with dust scraped off the columns that are inside the chapel, made a clay-like paste. Applied to the eyes this was meant to cure blindness in a precise re-enactment of a miracle of Jesus (*St John* 9.6-8).

Beuno's reputation for astounding miracles is best contemplated four miles on from Clynnog, at the village of Llanaelhaearn. Here the Ordnance Survey map indicates the whereabouts of 'Inscribed Stones' of archaeological significance, but this still requires a search. At the south corner of the churchyard, next to the road, there is an ancient monolith which now serves as a post marking the entrance to a driveway. If ever there was an inscription, it has long since disappeared. Likewise, in the burial ground there is a slender upright slab, distinctly early, but with no sign of lettering. To the right of the church path, however, a square-looking stone is clearly inscribed with the name 'Melitus', the date of which has been estimated at around AD500. And inside the church, set in the wall of the north transept, there is a somewhat longer stone of about the same age. This is to Aliortus a man 'from Elmet' (*Elmetiaco*) the early British kingdom that is now East Yorkshire (see Stones Appendix). The brief epitaph concludes with words which are frequently used to mark early Christian burials – *hic iacet*, 'here lies' or 'here he lies'.

These memorials are more primitive in appearance than that to Cadfan at Llangadwaladr and are certainly more typical of the post-Roman period. The inscriptions are simple and give the impression of a rather humble community. But that is not how the monks of Clynnog perceived this evidence of a literate history a mere four miles up the tracks and in a very prominent position. Painfully aware of their neighbours' superior claim to be the local founders of the only true faith, Beuno's followers hatched a story which would obscure the existence of this devout band of Christians who had settled near the Arfon coast a hundred years prior to their own arrival. To understand how they achieved their aim we need to look at a pattern in the more dramatic legends of the saint.

Nowhere is the wizard-like stature of Clynnog's founder more ecstatically proclaimed than in a cycle of resurrection stories, crafted in conformity with the pagan-Celtic perception of the human head as the seat of the soul. These cleverly targeted tales were intended to exalt Beuno as the star of the north even as David, patron saint of Wales, emerged as pre-eminent in the kingdoms of the south. The most well-known of them is set at Holywell and tells of the trauma which befell the northern saint's niece:

In expectation of refreshment while out hunting, Prince Caradog called at the home of Tyfid and his wife and was surprised to discover their daughter Winefride entirely alone. Her parents had gone to hear Beuno, a preacher of the word of God. Caradog sought to rape this child and she, forestalling his advances, took herself to her room then fled toward the church. Like a dog with its quarry, he pursued her to the threshold and drew out his sword. He dealt such a blow that the virgin's head fell to the floor in sight of the congregation. Beuno was seen to lift the head as he reverently pressed it to the girl's lifeless body before covering her with his cloak. He then implored her parents to hear out the mass and say prayers for her soul. Nor did Beuno fail to curse the offender, who melted like beeswax and was never seen again.

Coming from the church, Winefride's parents discovered to their astonishment that their daughter was alive, seated and sweating from her savage ordeal. About her neck there was a scar, and from the earth where her blood had fallen there gushed a clear fountain, Ffynnon Wenfrewi. Because of this miracle, Winefride devoted herself heart and mind to the service of Christ. She wove each winter a coat for her rescuer in gratitude for her life. This she placed on top of a boulder in the midst of a stream where Beuno used to pray, and from here it was carried to the shore at Clynnog. Such was her skill in making this garment that 'rain never wetted him, nor the wind moved his hair,' the saint was known by the name of 'dry cloak' (casul sych).

Another similar story makes a connection with Anglesey and the seat of royalty:

A high-born girl by the name of Digwg fell deeply in love with a lowly labourer from Aberffraw. Because this boy was fair and gentle her father, Ynyr Gwent, thought he must be a prince and insisted on giving him his daughter's hand in marriage. As the newly-weds rested on their return to a humble cottage, the groom fell into a deep despair. So darkly did he perceive their future together that he killed his beautiful bride, just as she was sleeping, to spare *her a life of utter degradation. Beuno's shepherds came upon the corpse not far from their monastery and summoned their master. He pressed the head to the lifeless body and resurrected Digwg with the power of prayer. From where her blood was spilt there arose a spring, henceforth known as Ffynnon Ddigwg.*

Having recounted two of these miracle legends, there is yet another in what was once a series of six or seven; apart from a few fragments the others were lost. Collected as a story in the eighteenth century, this third had the effect of sweeping the early Christian monuments set up at Llanaelhaearn firmly into the margins of a fanciful history. It makes the village appear to have been founded merely as an adjunct of Clynnog Fawr:

Beuno went each evening to pray where a stream-bound boulder served as his sanctuary. So much did he prefer this solitude that, catching sight of a persistent intruder and forgetful of that part of the office (I Peter 5.9) warning him against uncharitable thoughts, he invoked this spell:

> *'If well-intent, let no harm afflict he who thus regards me, otherwise let him suffer.'*

On the next evening there arose a commotion from the bank where the watcher lay concealed. Reaching that spot, Beuno found to his dismay one of his own dear monks, torn to pieces by a pack of wolves. He set to tending the victim's dismembered body and cared for him until he was whole again. There was, however, one disfigurement he could not disguise, a lost bone-shard of the monk's eyebrow. With iron Beuno fashioned a likeness and set it in the open wound. Henceforth his companion went by the name of Aelhaearn (Iron-brow). Aelhaearn chose not to abide in Clynnog but built a cell within sound of its bell so that he might continue in the hours of prayer.

The attribution to Beuno of this series of resurrection miracles makes his claim to a special status among the saints of North Wales somewhat unique. None other rejoices in a catalogue of such astonishing deeds. Further to this, the naming of settlements and landscape features after the disciples of a monastery's founder, whatever had happened to merit such an association, effectively captured the pre-existing sacredness in the countryside around. It was to make holy sites appear as if they had been newly established, rather than taken over, whether or not they were, originally, Christian or pagan. The imposition of a memorable story was an extension of this project, the hero himself being placed in the limelight; not leaving to chance that the name of the disciple alone would forever bring to mind the identity of his mentor. With the legend of Aelhaearn, Clynnog successfully eclipsed the earliest Christian history of the site which is today known only as Llanaelhaearn. Similarly, in the account of Digwg's resurrection, the saint's spiritual supremacy was boldly asserted in connection with the royal household at Aberffraw.

At Holywell this formula proved so remarkably effective that in time it backfired and with an unforeseen consequence. Instead of impressing the hearers with Beuno, the legend provoked unstoppable sympathy for the object of his compassion: the female whose role was to appear more or less helpless – no more than his seamstress! By the twelfth century, Winefride's cult had gained momentum and in 1398 was so much in the ascendant that by order of Canterbury her feast was made obligatory (3 November). Richard II went on a pilgrimage to Holywell. Henry V made a similar journey before setting out for France. His victory at Agincourt, in 1415, was down to Welsh bowmen who had trained in the marchers. Following the battle the king went to Shrewsbury to venerate Winefride's relics before walking barefoot, fifty miles north, to the miraculous pool; to this day one of the Seven Wonders of Wales. Although there are more churches dedicated to Beuno than to any other saint throughout North Wales, to complement David, Saint of the South, it was not Beuno but Winefride who, by popular acclaim was chosen to be the most honoured Saint of the North. This rebuff to Beuno's reputation has had its repercussions to the present day. Unlike St David's at the tip of Pembrokeshire, the church at Clynnog draws barely a trickle of visitors. The stories constructed for its illustrious founder seem not to have had the desired effect.

Llangybi Well House

CHAPTER 5

CYBI'S WELL

LLANGYBI

Away from the major roads and holiday resorts there are, amid the hills of the Llŷn peninsula, villages of remarkable beauty and old world charm. One such is Llangybi, a scatter of houses beside the country lanes that run like threads of a spider's web around the wooded hillside of Garn Bentyrch. In this inland location *ynys* is not an island but a riverside meadow with its lush green sward. Before the enclosures and the patterning of fields, the land around Llangybi was a primordial Eden made ready for cultivation and year-round grazing, interspersed with the harvests that could easily be garnered from its game-filled woods and innumerable streams. The land today has lost none of its enchantment.

The single chambered village church is fifteenth century, extensively repaired in Victorian times and made somewhat notorious in the 1960s for having been stripped of its medieval frescoes. Fortunately retained is a seventh century cross incised on an upright slab to the left of the lych-gate, the earliest indication of the boundary of the *llan*. At the far corner of the burial ground, to the left of the church, a stone stile marks the beginning of an indistinct path heading straight down the fields. This leads to some steps and a tree-lined trackway where, almost opposite, there is a kissing-gate to a foot-bridge and, looking beyond, a triangular field at the end of which, beneath a wooded hillside, is an ancient well house next to the shell of a keeper's cottage.

In the summer of 1766 Diederick Wessel Linden MD, a world authority on curative waters, stayed a while at Llangybi and took a sample from Cybi's Well. He tested that it was alkaline and under a microscope observed specks of what he noted as 'fine white metallic earth'. For Linden this confirmed a general belief that the water was from an aquifer in rock-embedded silver beneath the summit of Garn Bentyrch. His curiosity aroused, he went on to examine a log of impressive cures at the well in the care of the Reverend RF Williams, rector of Llanystumdwy. This seemingly sober document convinced the doctor that the liquid on his specimen glass possessed 'virtues of which all other waters now known in Great Britain are destitute'. It had apparently restored sight to several invalids made blind by the effects of the terrifying smallpox. One of these patients was a man called Sion Rhydderch who had been without vision for at least thirty years. Within a few weeks, Linden had published an interim report in *The Gentleman's Magazine* trumpeting the arrival of what he described as 'a sure remedy in all disorders of the eyes'. No sooner had this article gone into circulation than sales of cottage-bottled Cybi Water required what can only be described as a near industrial scale of production, particularly when reinforced by traditional claims that here there was also a cure for dermatitis, rheumatism and tuberculosis.

The choice of a popular English periodical in which to break the news of this amazing discovery was determined by an understanding that the inhabitants of Llangybi would improve their guardianship of what then appeared, potentially, to be a world-class spa. Fired with enthusiasm for a new kind of health tourism, they directed their efforts to making sure that the grim looking clutter from previous exploitations of the well was promptly disposed of. Crutches for the lame and medieval wheelbarrows to carry the infirm were all gathered up and quickly destroyed. Unlike injured farm workers, quarrymen and other locals who had enjoyed the benefits of Llangybi in the past, the better class of visitor would be enfeebled and partially sighted from far too much reading. Above all other considerations, they would also be exceedingly wealthy and generous to a fault. Such a clientele needed to be led to the well, singly or in couples, in a quiet and orderly fashion. They would not suffer being trucked and herded in a noisy jolly crowd on saints' holy days as had long been the tradition. An antique chest for monetary offerings, in thanksgiving for 'miracles', known locally as Cyff Gybi, was spirited out of the church and not seen thereafter. Not a penny was to be misdirected.

In spite of these reforms, the regeneration of Llangybi was not a success. Linden's plan that the village 'be accommodated with proper habitations for those that have occasion to resort to it,' was a dream too far. Just one guest house continued to be more than adequate despite the publicity; the spate of enthusiasm died, it seems, as suddenly as it had flared, due no doubt to the moderate effects of the only slightly impure water. One senses desperation in at least one entry in the log: William Sion Thomas, employed locally as a tailor, was relieved of the inconvenience of 'a sharp pain in the nose'. The cure of minor ailments was not what Linden had optimistically envisaged. Despite efforts to the contrary Cybi's Well had survived an Age of Science and Reason almost unscathed. The entire site is now in the care of Cadw.

The main pool is in a room built of un-mortared walls at the top of which are the remains of what appears to be corbelled vaulting. This structure has been consolidated over time but has all the features which would suggest that it existed roughly in its present form from before the Reformation. Water flows in from a smaller pool set in a rectangular room to the rear of this building, certainly the oldest part and generally referred to as the eye of the well. A pavement surrounds the main pool and the walls have niches where bathers would rest between several immersions, morning and night for seven to ten days. Local folklore tells of a friendly eel that slithers from the depths and coils around anyone blessed with a cure. Although this seems highly improbable, there is a tradition of tipping eels into wells to serve as cleaner-fish, ridding the water of organic impurities.

Converging on the well-house are two ancient stone track-ways and beside one of these is the *gofer*, Welsh for an 'outflow'. Combining health with reverie, the visitor may paddle in this bubbling little stream while admiring the view; a valley of marsh pastures utterly serene and bounded on every side by the sheltering trees. Although Cybi's famous monastery was in the fort at Caergybi, this peaceful scene chimes perfectly with his sacred legends and the credible suggestion that this scion of Cornish nobility came to live

Ffynnon Gybi

here along with his friends after a pilgrimage to the Holy Land, some years spent at Poitiers and a visit to Ireland.

There are three places in Wales where land commemorating Cybi lies within a few miles of dedications to a lesser known saint called Gwyndaf: Capel Gwyndaf, Llanwnda (Pembrokeshire) and ten miles north of Llangybi, the village of Llanwnda. This suggests a longstanding connection between two monastic families, possibly one of rivalry dating back to the sixth century when Cybi was alive. A memory of conflict has certainly survived in a tale apparently transposed to Ireland by an anonymous monk of the thirteenth century who wrote *Vita Sancti Kebii*, an account of Cybi's life. Here the equivalent of Gwyndaf was a trickster called Fintan. The story begins in an ominous fashion, with a metaphor representing an infringement of land rights. The stage is set by the sight of a beast rampaging unhindered through ripened corn. This minor incident sets in train a series of events which imperil the life of Cybi's uncle, an ascetic saint of the church at Llangefni:

Cyngar, a man of noble birth, lived a life of penitence. He wore a shirt of goat's hair, ate barley-bread and prayed standing in cold water. Great was his knowledge of the world of nature; he turned marshlands into fields and planted yew trees. Kings paid their respects to him out of a fear of offending God. As he grew old Cyngar could no longer eat solid food. It was then that Cybi, his nephew, son of Selyf and friend of Seiriol, bought a cow in calf for his relative in order that he might live. When the calf was born the cow gave milk both for its offspring and the old man.

Cyngar's cow was tethered but not its calf. This little beast wandered into the harvest of Fintan who had long been upset by Maelog, one of Cybi's closest disciples. All who cultivated land with Cybi did so as if in an ecstasy, not least of them his dear Maelog, whose ploughing as far as Fintan's threshold had offended the man. Fintan tethered the calf to a tree and refused to release it; Cyngar's cow ceased lactation and the saint began to starve.

Eschewing violence, Cybi turned to prayer. As he arose from his meditations, it was God's justice that opened his eyes. He saw the calf racing toward him, dragging the tree by its gargantuan roots.

Just as St Beuno's sanctity was attested by birds – a form of ornithomancy – St Cybi's claims to land were validated with the co-operation of beasts of pasture. His competency in this respect was buttressed with yet another rather convoluted story, a paradigm of which occurs in an oral tradition at Llaneilian on Anglesey: St Eilian's cattle were taken quite brazenly by authority of King Cadwallon. In righteous retribution Eilian struck the king with blindness. This curse was only lifted when the offended saint won all the revenues from land encompassed by a deer put to flight from the royal hunt. Such a strange competition is mirrored in an argument devised for an earlier time between Cybi and King Maelgwn who, as we have seen already, was Cadwallon's ancestor. The description of the prize is tantalisingly vague. The word 'promontory' could mean Ynys Gybi, the north-western island of the Isle of Anglesey, or the entire Llŷn peninsula; and the quarry on this occasion is a female goat. The scribe brings into play a painful family grievance which also allows Cybi, with equal vehemence, to call down a curse:

It came to pass one day that King Maelgwn went into the hills to hunt and seeing a she-goat set his molossus at her. (So called because the dogs of Molossis in Epirus were famed for their size and ferocity.) This goat ran swiftly for refuge to Cybi whose cousin, Caffo, brother of Gildas and founder of Llangaffo monastery, had been killed by the shepherds of the royal town of Rhosyr. Cybi had cursed these murderers along with their wanton mistress. With crass indifference to the saint's finer feelings Maelgwn sought the goat's release. 'I will not leave go of her,' said Cybi, 'unless you spare her life.' Hearing this, the king became exceedingly annoyed: 'If you do not obey me I will throw you off this land.' To which Cybi replied: 'It is not in your power to throw me off this land; that is for God alone. However, for your sake I will abandon this goat to you if you will offer up the land she shall have encircled when chased by your molossus.' To this the king assented. The goat was duly released, whence Maelgwn's hunting-dog followed her throughout the entire promontory. After this long and exhausting pursuit she returned and sought refuge of her peaceful protector.

With its holy well, Llangybi rightly enjoys its modest reputation as a place of historic interest, yet Cybi's legends are seldom recalled. The saint has even been damned because of them. An otherwise admirable scholar, Canon Gilbert Doble, lambasted the *Vita* for being 'feeble and insipid … puerile and absolutely worthless.' But it was not the purpose of these sacred legends to fulfil a notional criterion of literary merit. Nor were they, in Cybi's case, simply an explanation for revenues from property. There was rather a need for the promulgation of a popular history: the sort that could be seen to commend the Church to a devoutly pagan society. Christian scriptures describe a landscape with cedars, fig trees, spice bushes and well pools set in the heart of a teeming city. This mysterious imagery would have been alien to the inhabitants of Gwynedd. Stories of known pastures, familiar trees, country wells and solitary *llannau*, were compensation for the unfamiliar setting of the exotic Gospels. In this respect there is a delightful tale that illustrates the dilemma with a touching compassion.

Among the legends of Gwynedd there is the story of Tysilio, a prince whose teacher was a venerable scholar by the name of Gwyddfarch. Tysilio rejected his right to rule Powys in order to become a hermit on Church Island in the Menai Strait. No moment is more poignant for localised faith than when, out of consideration for Gwyddfarch's infirmities, Tysilio turned down the suggestion of a pilgrimage to Rome. Instead, slowly and patiently, he walked his frail mentor onto the Welsh mountains, after which experience the old man rested and simply dreamed of the holy city. It could not possibly be more beautiful than the pastures and the wilderness through which he had been led.

Holy Cross Church, Llannor

CHAPTER 6

FIGULINUS'S PLEA
TO A HEAVENLY MATHEMATICIAN

LLANNOR

Six miles west of Llangybi, just north of Pwllheli, another quiet settlement stretches out along the banks of streams and in the shelter of a shallow valley. Llannor probably receives its name from a corruption of *llan-fawr*, 'great llan'. As if to confirm this, the church with its gaunt tower stands very prominently in a raised burial ground at the centre of the village. Access for visitors is by prior arrangement with the vicar. Llannor is not on the tourist trail and few people are aware that the church contains anything out of the ordinary. A thirteenth century nave and chancel has wall plaques to local families and makes mention of their part in the glory days of empire. But distanced from these polished memorials, inside the main entrance, there is a sombre upright stone with holes bored at one end. It was at one time a gatepost, but where bolts used to penetrate there is a Latin inscription.

Four post-Roman epitaph stones have come to light from the parish of Llannor; one of them has been lost. Of the three that remain, two are columns of basalt, hexagonal in cross-section. These are on display at Plas Glyn y Weddw, an Art Gallery at Llanbedrog. Down the side of one is carved a name, Vendesetl. The other reads:

IOVENALI FILI ETERNI HIC IACIT
'(stone) of-Ieuan son of-Edern; here he-lies'.

The significance of these inscriptions will become clear in due course. For now, it is the stone at Llannor which turns out to be the more surprising.

There is an unfortunate prejudice against post-Roman Latin epitaphs which sees them as little more than feeble imitations of monuments of the Roman period. Such an impression may have taken a hold on the reader at first sight of those to be found at Llanaelhaearn. They appear to be not in any way sophisticated and are, for the most part, carved on undressed stone. In Britain these seemingly simple memorials have only ever been found at the northerly and westerly limits of formerly Roman occupied territory. There are two on the Isle of Man, a dozen in the south of Scotland, some fifty in Devon and Cornwall, and more than one hundred and eighty at locations throughout Wales. The Latin is frequently said to be symptomatic of a decline of literacy and, to be fair, many of the inscriptions look as if they had been rather poorly crafted; the stone to Cadfan at Llangadwaladr is a notable exception. What, if anything, can recommend a memorial so unprepossessing that it was removed, from what ever was its original position, to hold up a gate? Somewhat ungrammatically (with repetitive genitives) the inscription reads:

Left: *Total numbers of post-Roman inscribed stones for each of their area of origin. Dots indicate the whereabouts of those 'known or suspected' to be in biblical style*
Right: *Figulinus Stone*

FIGVLINI FILI LOCVLITI HIC IACIT
'(stone) of-Figulinus, son of-Loculitus; here he-lies'.

These names are culturally Roman and would have had similar origins to our present day surnames: *figulus* means a potter. It does not imply, however, that the deceased ever pursued such an occupation. It is not the name that is interesting but how the words are set out. (What follows is a simplified treatment, based on Thomas – 1998 – but with a different conclusion.) Rather than carved down the length of the stone they are confined to one end. The reason has to do with their 'biblical' style.

As Roman authority weakened in the late fourth century, a learned monk in Palestine set about combating the threat of religious disunity with a Bible written entirely in Latin (it is known as the 'Vulgate'). Working from texts in Greek and Hebrew, St Jerome, 'Prince of Translators', constructed certain word patterns for the further edification of his well-schooled readers. One method of achieving such a nuanced aim is to employ the alphabet as a substitute for numbers. (Latin always had this dual usage, the obvious instance being in Roman numerals.) Bearing this in mind, let us look again at the inscription on display in the porch at Llannor.

The alphabet in Roman and post-Roman times was more often than not twenty letters. KYZ were mainly only ever used in older Latin and just occasionally in the Vulgate, JWU were medieval additions, U being a variant of the letter V. Suppose the letters of this slimmed down series are given sequential numbers:

A B C D E F G H I L M N O P Q R S T V X
1 2 3 4 5 6 7 8 9 10 11 12 13 14 15 16 17 18 19 20

Carved almost entirely in capitals, the layout at Llannor, for all its appearance of epitaphical naivety, seems to have been arranged to give emphasis everywhere to multiples of three (see over page for outline):

As well as being set out in three lines, the left hand marginal letters F L H add up to 24, right hand marginals I I T add up to 36. Not only is the first letter of the inscription number 6, but the first line ends having made six syllables. Enthusiasts for puzzles will entertain the thought that all this is a clue. Ought the text to be reconfigured as having three sides, in which case it turns out to be an equilateral triangle? In this shape the marginal totals add up to 144, a very significant Christian number:

6	F	6
9	I G	7
19	V L I	9
12	N I F I	9
10	L I L O C	3
19	V L I T I H	8
9	I C I A C I T	18
84	+	60
	= 144	

(reproduced courtesy of Thomas, CC, 1998)

Revelation, the last book of the Bible, is devoted to a prophecy of the world's final days. In a highly imaginative scene, the walls of the new Jerusalem, established for eternity, are described as having a height of 144 cubits. The number of souls divinely pre-ordained to dwell within the city is 144,000 (*Revelation* 14.1 & 21.17). The inscription has suggested that Figulinus ought to be among these lucky citizens. The points of the triangle also combine to make another key number: I F T = 33, the supposed age of Jesus on the day of his crucifixion. Figulinus is associated with the suffering of his Saviour in the belief that, along with the penitent crucified next to Jesus (*St Luke* 23.39-43) he too will be told that he is destined for heaven.

Like the uppermost carvings on the Trajan monument in the heart of Rome, beyond the sight of ground-based mortals, the key numbers at Llannor are not to impress us, but a celestial intelligence, albeit the inscription was set close to the grave. Mathematics was the heavenly science; the epitaph therefore was appropriately devised. Let us enter the imagination of a sixth century Christian, albeit one who was learned. In the final days of Earth, an angel descends from the sky attracted by *hic iacit*, 'here lies', a phrase

Figulinus Inscription, outline

common on important Christian graves, on this occassion with the not unusual alternative spelling of *iacet*. Closer inspection reveals that the letters are carefully aligned for a biblical style. On this monument, pinpointing the place where a soul awaits resurrection is all the evidence an advocate requires to plead his case: 'This was a man whose intelligent Christian friends thought him worthy of Paradise'. What a pity for Figulinus that the stone, it seems, has been not just once, but twice relocated!

Pistyll

CHAPTER 7

THE PILGRIM PATH
PISTYLL AND LLANGWNNADL

Four miles north and slightly west of Llannor, the coast road down the north side of the Llŷn peninsula makes a sharp bend into a valley on the west side of Gwylfa. Just below this road there is a National Trust car park. From here one can easily walk the short distance down the lane to where St Beuno's monks diverted a waterfall (*pistyll*) to create a fish pond. It can be seen that their dam was later reinforced to provide the power for a mill race, but any wheel and its housing have since been removed; the pond has gone wild with a raft of aquatic weeds. Directly opposite there is a curvilinear wall, the boundary of what used to be a small Celtic monastery. This too has long since disappeared, leaving a small twelfth century church with a large burial ground.

Entering this building one feels a sudden sense of the suspension of time. As with many a remote Welsh church there is no electricity: whatever light there is, is natural. The sea facing wall has only one small window so as to form a barrier against the prevailing wind; it looks onto the altar for the benefit of the leprous who were excluded from entering but were permitted to observe mass. A powerful grassy fragrance hangs in the air from the carpet of rushes strewn across the nave, a tradition from the time when the floor was bare earth. Dated by their shallow pitch, the roof beams are sixteenth century and appear as if calcified by the effects of the sea air. The sanctuary here is late medieval and prominently displays a post-Reformation fragment of plaster showing a biblical text: *Clodforwch yr Arglwydd canys da yw*, 'Praise the Lord, for he is good' (Psalm 107). Older than the nave and close to the door there is a font of the late tenth or the eleventh century, carved with a Manx design of overlapping double ovals interwoven all around with horizontal bands. To the illiterate attender at an infant baptism this particular Celtic pattern spelt 'Eternal Life'.

It is surmised that Beuno chose the Pistyll valley for his Lenten retreats. A line of fields to the north offers a shelf for gentle walking and the persistence of dwarf elderberry in parts of the burial ground suggests there was at one time a medicinal herb garden. In summer, the monastery would have been a place of refreshment for pilgrims heading south-west in the direction of Bardsey, along what is now the route of the B4417. At the base of the left hand wall, about 100 yards beyond the lay-by, three quarters of a mile along this road, there is an incised ringed cross (co-ordinates 319 418) one of the small marker stones that used to be in the fields as a simple reassurance to those hoping to reach the holy and, as yet, invisible island. Bardsey seems to have been elevated to the same sacred status as Compostela, city of the reliquary of St James the Apostle, in North West Spain. By 1120 it was known as 'the Rome of Britain'; three trips to the island conferred the same spiritual benefit as a pilgrimage across Europe to the Eternal City.

St Beuno's Church, Pistyll

Continuing down the coast road, a little beyond Morfa Nefyn we come to the village of Edern. Translated into Latin, as we have seen already, this spells Eternus, the name on one of the Llannor stones at Plas Glyn y Weddw. The church here is Victorian but it is set in a raised and partly circular burial ground, a site almost certainly consecrated in the post-Roman period.

Seven miles further on, beyond Tudweiliog, there is a lane off to the right down a *cwm* to Llangwnnadl, *llan* of Gwynhoedl, 'He of the Shining Life'; a somewhat ironic name as, according to genealogy, this saint was one among five, all sons of Seithenyn who was a byword for infamy. The brothers were Tudglyd, Tudno of Llandudno, Senewyr and Merin, the saint of a ruined church two and a half miles away on the approach to Porth Ferin. Seithenyn stands forever condemned in mythology as the drunken Lord of (Cantref) Gwaelod, a valuable marsh pasture in Cardigan Bay. At least it was until it was deluged because of his failure to maintain the sea dyke. The name Vendesetl on the second stone at Glyn y Weddw is a Latin form of Gwynhoedl. (It is anyone's guess how both these memorials came to be either side of what was, apparently, a pagan grave – *ie* orientated north-south rather than east-west – in a field at Penprys in the parish of Llannor).

From the path to the main entrance, Llangwnnadl Church looks deceptively small. It was once similar in size to Pistyll but considerably enlarged early in the sixteenth century when the side aisles were built. This task was undertaken in confident anticipation of the new space being thronged with enthusiastic pilgrims. Arabesque lettering on one of the piers of the arcading authoritatively informs us *S. Gwynhoydyl iacet hic*, 'St Gwynhoedl lies here'. Carved a thousand years after the saint had died, the words show no doubt as to the location of his remains. In the south aisle wall, about twelve feet from the door, there is a very large undressed stone feintly inscribed with a circled cross. Powdered red dye is still visible in the grooves. Dated to around AD600 this was perhaps, along with the Vendesetl pillar, a boulder which first marked Gwynhoedl's grave. What better use for such a crude looking memorial than to bulk out the wall stone behind a screed of plaster? Out of sight for three hundred years, it only came to light when the plaster was stripped off, throughout the interior, in 1952.

An intriguing curiosity is usually kept in the chancel, in the form of a hand bell which visitors may ring. This is the replica of an original from the time when the village supported a school with classes in the church. The real bell went missing but turned up in an auction where it went under the hammer for £44. Expert opinion has come to the conclusion that it was made in the tenth century and happens to be the largest copper-alloy casting of its kind in Wales. In the interests of security, the real Llangwnnadl bell is now in Cardiff, in the National Museum. Such bells were rung at the celebration of mass, but regarded with suspicion as magical and tricksy. According to one story, Gildas fashioned just such a bell for the delight of St David but it stubbornly refused to work. Only when it was passed to the learned Abbot Illtud did it emit a beautiful sound.

As the last overnight stop before a final day's walk to the sea, and then the crossing to Bardsey, Llangwnnadl Church must at times have been the scene of an intense excitement. We can appreciate a pilgrim's feelings from some lines of a poem in the *Black Book of Carmarthen*, a thirteenth century collection of what is undoubtedly material from an earlier time:

Y mae vimrid ar debed	My mind is set on a journey
arowun ar mor wyned	My intent is to put to sea.
etyl butic bytaud ked.	A beneficial plan, a gift it will be.
Ystarn de wineu fruin guin	Saddle the bay with white nostrils
redech hiraethauc raun rin	Eager to run, with a rough coat.
ren new oet reid duu genhin.	King of Heaven, we would need God's aid.

The pilgrims' campsite and tethering for pack animals was across the river from the church, in a field known to this day as *cae eisteddfa*, 'the place of sitting'.

On another of the piers in the north arcade is carved the date 1520, the year of the commencement of work to enlarge the church. But all was not well. Monks on Bardsey who had organised this project were in for a rude awakening. By the 1530s Henry VIII's distressed marriage had made urgent the need for a complete break from Rome. With astonishing speed the king's agents closed all monasteries and declared an end to pilgrimages wherever they took place. Religious enthusiasts roaming the countryside were not to be tolerated, lest they took advantage of an established tradition as cover for a rebellion.

On the Llŷn peninsula the Reformation was a bolt from the blue. In the previous one hundred and fifty years, in addition to St Gwynhoedl's, four churches had been enlarged in an unshakeable belief that religious tourism had a glorious future: Clynnog Fawr, Llanengan, Abererch and Aberdaron. This investment suddenly appeared extremely ill advised. As if to mock the monks' ambitions, the interior at Llangwnnadl had not only been adorned with costly octagonal piers and recessed inscriptions – raised lettering in countersunk panels – but also a reminder of who was really in charge. On the sides of a font, which no doubt replaced one of the Celtic style, no longer in fashion, is yet more expensive and sycophantic carving: a likeness of Skeffington, Bishop of Bangor, identified by his mitre and, on the opposite side, one of the young King Henry, not so much smiling as truculently smirking, the author of economic disaster, or so it seemed, here in Llangwnnadl in the sixteenth century. A beautiful church was hardly compensation for the permanent loss of pilgrimages and the money they brought in.

As Wales was increasingly obliged to embrace Protestantism, rituals of the Middle Ages faded from memory. One consequence of this is that the paths trodden by pilgrims can no longer be accurately traced. The way from Llangwnnadl may have been toward Bryncroes to connect with a south pilgrimage route starting from Tywyn. From Bryncroes there would have been a trackway to the entrance of the *clas* monastery which at one time occupied most of Aberdaron. Another ancient path may underlie what is now a country lane leading to Capel Anelog and the site of a Christian cemetery of the fifth or sixth century. Not far from Anelog is

Braich y Pwll, supposedly the oldest place of embarkation for Bardsey on the west side of Uwchmynydd, the 'Further Mountain'. Here on land owned by the National Trust are the foundations of a building that may have been a chapel. Among the tidal rocks below this landmark there is a spring, Ffynnon Fair, 'St Mary's Well', where the voyagers are said to have filled their flasks. But this is pure conjecture. What is known for certain is that from wherever they sailed, the thought of crossing to Bardsey filled most pilgrims with dread. Many had never set foot in a boat before and their destination had a cautionary name, Ynys Enlli (*ynys yn y llif*) 'island in the flood-tide'. A legend of Powys describes the terror that overcame a family from a village near St Asaph. They journeyed this far and dared go no further until a familial saint rushed to their aid. Appearing like Moses before the Red Sea, their relative Mordeyrn (Môr-teyrn, 'Sea-sovereign') had first to find a magical beast, yellow as the rock (*maen melyn*) which is a quartzite crystal unique to the cliffs on the west side of Uwchmynydd:

Mordeyrn possessed such powers of healing that made Nantglyn known throughout the country as a wonderful place. The sight of his countenance alone cured the illnesses of many in pain and their animals too. Long after his lifetime, turf from this village was sold as if it were medicine for sick and diseased cattle. This son of Eurdeyrn was of a family that planned a pilgrimage, for the merit of their kinsfolk and all whom they loved. So it was that they set out for Enlli. Mordeyrn would not join them but promised he would follow.

They walked to a stone which leaned to the island, where for fear of the sea, they would venture no further. Only then did Mordeyrn appear, sat on a colt with a bright yellow coat. He parted the waves and followed them across. As the tide turned and covered their causeway, the hooves of his colt, though dry and trembling, sent splinters of sunlight to the swirling deep.

Bardsey Island

CHAPTER 8

SENACUS CAUGHT IN A NET

BARDSEY ISLAND AND ABERDARON

Bardsey takes its name from the seafarer Bardr, a Viking who laid claim to the island, probably in the ninth or the tenth century. From the mainland its appearance is of a mountain in the sea, somewhat dark and forbidding. But behind this rugged aspect there are a hundred small fields, a lighthouse, cottages, a farm and a thirteenth century tower, the only building from what was, five hundred years ago, an Augustinian monastery. Today the island has just eight permanent residents and is owned by a trust. This organisation aims to strike a balance between human activity and the abundant bird life; thousands of Manx sheerwater scoop out their burrows high upon the mountain where they rear their young within sound of the waves; late at night there is an eerie din on the island, an unearthly and chilling sound which the adults make as they return from feeding far out at sea. A day visit to Bardsey is dependant on calm weather. A ferry from Porth Meudwy, the 'Hermit's Cove' on the east side of Uwchmynydd, crosses the straits to *y cafn*, 'the trough', a tidal slipway among the rocks and grey seals.

Inside a Victorian chapel on Bardsey there is a stone carved with a cross and part of a cross-shaft with the lower half of a monk in a pleated robe. During the Reformation any shrines were destroyed and these are the only fragments of medieval art. The twelfth century *Book of Llandaff* cites the island as the resting place of twenty thousand saints, but none has a name from the numerous graves located thus far. A late medieval tradition makes Cadfan the first abbot, not the immoral king but the patron saint of Tywyn in the fifth or sixth century. Epitaphs from that period have been found on the mainland and are now at Aberdaron, in a church said to have been founded by two of Cadfan's followers, the monks Hywyn and Lleuddad.

There is a *Buchedd Llewddog Sant*, Book of St Lleuddad – the more probable first abbot – some rather strange anecdotes collected from a variety of sources and brought together in the sixteenth century: the young man, a son of Dingad ap Nudd Hael, King of Usk, secretly began paying visits to Bardsey where his brother, Baglan, was already a monk. It was he who appointed Hywyn to watch over the wanderer and to carry his 'holy bell'. Cadfan, when he heard of this, commanded Lleuddad to observe stability or else leave the island for good. He apparently obeyed and by the time of Cadfan's death the other clergy were jealous that their master had chosen the maverick, no less, to be his successor. At *cae bryn baglau*, 'field of the hill of staffs,' Lleuddad joined their staves so that only he could separate them. In another demonstration of his power to act as their leader, a quantity of milk was thrown into a well, probably *ffynnon y dalar*, a healing 'spring at the top of the ploughed field.' The test was to recover it. Except for Lleuddad none could achieve this miracle, but for him the *ffynnon* ran pure leaving the milk to flow separately. Toward the end of his life, Lleuddad obtained from God a promise that his monks would only ever die in succession of old age, and that *i'r iâ nid â'r un da*, 'not one good person would go to the ice.' These wishes were granted only on condition that the monks remained virtuous. For centuries, the believers, clergy and laity, those who had wealth enough for the final journey, were buried on Bardsey in the hope of participating in this assurance of peace.

Sheltered by an arc of hills and facing due south, Aberdaron is out of sight of the island, the most westerly and, by its appearance, the most idiosyncratic of the villages in Llŷn. 'There are no streets ... houses are scattered here and there as though some giant hand had rolled them down the hillside like dice, until at the bottom, at the edge of the sea, they came together in a clutch' (Byron Rogers). As well as a pub, a hotel and a tin hut bakery, according to the *Rough Guide*, just over the bridge, there is a fourteenth century pilgrims' hostel, Cegin Fawr, 'Great Kitchen'. This whitened house which is now a teashop dates in fact from the seventeenth century and behind it stands the equally age-deceptive Old Post Office designed in 1950 by Clough Williams-Ellis. Old St Hywyn's Church is close by the beach. This at least is genuine: twelfth century on the north side with a Romanesque west doorway and an east wall charmingly half buried in the sands. Without a priest for several years, St Hywyn's came into the charge of the Reverend Evelyn Davies who saved this building from an impending catastrophe. In the year 2000, she was persuaded to come to Aberdaron by the recurrence of a dream which kept showing her the church in a state of disrepair. Shortly after her

St Hywyn's Church, West Door

induction, an architect informed her that the south aisle wall was heading out to sea – the organiser of a rescue had arrived just in time! The poet RS Thomas was vicar of the parish from 1967 to 1978. Thanks to his diligence the two slender Llannor stones (ch 6) were recovered from a basement of the Ashmolean Museum and put on display at Plas Glyn y Weddw. Beautifully inscribed on their water-worn surfaces there is another pair of stones in St Hywyn's chancel. These were discovered a mile away at Capel Anelog, in a field at the head waters of Afon Sant. Dating from around AD500, each records the burial of a priest (*presbiter*) a title abbreviated to the letters PBR and PRSB. Although the inscriptions are in a sophisticated mid European style – letters embellished with serifs and the bar of letters A angled downwards – compilers of the Gwynedd handbook (1995) point out that the composer was none too literate. Nothing could be more untrue. Any irregularities are here carefully contrived just as at Llannor and Llangadwaladr.

Re-adjusting the word order for our translation the shorter of the epitaphs reads:

VERACIUS PBR HIC IACIT

'Veracius a-priest lies here'

In these few words there are apparently no hidden depths (but see Thomas, *CC*, 1998, fig 53). However, the longer of the two, having started in a similar fashion, offers more information with three more lines and some artfully fused letters. Opening up the ligatures the inscription reads word for word:

SENACUS PRSB HIC IACIT CUM MULTITUDINEM FRATRUM

'Senacus a-priest, here lies, with a-multitude of-the-brethren'

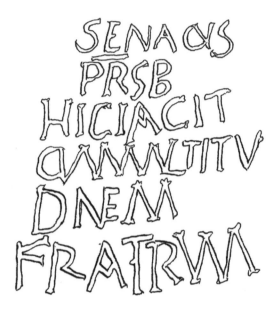

Senacus Inscription, outline

This suggests there are more burials at Anelog awaiting the possibility of an archaeological dig. Meanwhile, grammar dictates that *cum* ought really to take an ending in the ablative case. The word for a multitude should read *multitudine*, without the addition of a final letter *m*. Again we have a clue, remembering that some inscriptions have biblical style. For graduates of a monastic school this apparent 'misspelling' was a clear evocation.

The heart of *St Luke's* gospel (5.4-7) has Jesus on one occasion urging Simon Peter to continue trawling in the Sea of Galilea even though he and his weary companions had toiled through the night in vain. The disciple consented, only to discover that their net then entrapped *piscium multitudinem copiosam*, 'a plentiful swarm of fishes'. The ungrammatical epitaph now has its reference! The hidden prayer for Senacus is the same as that for Figulinus on the more crude looking stone beside the door of Llannor Church. Here in Aberdaron it is stated in reference to a boat of salvation, an image not uncommon in religious art throughout the Middle Ages. On the day of judgement, Senacus will be hauled heavenward, along with fellow Christians, like fish caught in a net cast by an order of their Saviour. Mynydd Anelog is on the coast. From the mountain it is credible that the priests and their brethren might claim to see swarms of fish, particularly the grey mullet, invisible at sea level. In other words, they would transfer to a knowledge of their own landscape a second account of the story in the *Gospel of St John* (21.4-6) this time with Jesus standing on the shore, directing the disciples as to the whereabouts of the shoal.

Senacus is so full of allusion that it can confidently be asserted that none of its contortions are merely the product of a semi-literate mind. The ligatures support this. In line five, the merging of I with N makes DNE, widely used shorthand in Latin for *Domine*, 'Lord'; both biblical versions of the story of the net conclude with a revelation of Jesus as Lord. An unabbreviated model of the whole inscription shows up the heavenly number in end of line additions, just as at Llannor, but in this instance concealed by the style of texting (*ie* reduction) rather than by any reconfiguration of the shape:

Line 1	17	S E N A C U S	17
Line 2	14	P R e S B i t e r	16
Line 3	8	H I C I A C I T	18
Line 4	3	C U M M U L T I T U	19
Line 5	4	D I N E M	11
Line 6	6	F R A T R U M	11
	52	+	92
		= 144	

(reproduced courtesy of Thomas, CC, 1998)

For a better understanding of this complicated epitaph than space here permits, the reader needs to consult the relevant pages of archaeologist Charles Thomas's book *Christian Celts*. Along with Figulinus, Senacus is a work of considerable ingenuity; it bears comparison with devices in the texts of other world faiths: in cabbalistic lore, numbers correspond with letters in Hebrew and Aramaic and, from these, are abstracted esoteric subtexts by substituting words of the same numerical value. The 'perilous journey to heaven' likewise has its parallel in the 'journey to an afterlife' written in hieroglyphs in the tombs of the Pharaohs. In Senacus and Figulinus we see not only the Roman tradition but several themes that characterise the faiths of the Near East.

Shifting our concentration away from the stone to the interior of St Hywyn's, we can become aware of the stillness that pervades this church so close to the sea. Suppressed by the thickness of the south aisle wall, noises from the beach are reduced to a whisper. Outside, in the daylight, the same quietness attends five ancient sites (see Appendices) south of the road from Aberdaron to Llanbedrog. On Rhiw Mountain there are two little known holy wells: one in a field above Plas yn Rhiw and another in the forest from where the *ffynnon* runs fast, in the manner of a flume; there is a third in a garden in the village of Llanengan. A mile to the north of here lies Llangian churchyard, its vast flock of headstones making yet more discreet the faint inscription to a sixth century physician. From where there is a view of St Tudwal's Islands, high on Mynytho Common, there is a fourth holy well, Ffynnon Fyw, a spring softly arising from the sloping ground and setting on its course through the gorse and the bracken.

Traeth Llanddwyn

CONCLUSION

The exact date has not been ascertained, but at some time in or around AD560 there had been an ongoing disunity in a meeting of bishops at Llanddewibrefi in Ceredigion. One of the younger brethren was persuaded to come forward, at which point the ground rose beneath his feet so that everyone could see him. He delivered a sermon which condemned Pelagius, an exponent of good works as a means of salvation. This intervention showed the eloquence of St David who, from that point on seemed unassailable. A thousand years later there were fifty churches and chapels bearing his name, all in the south, and it can be justly said that the great saints of the north were even then in the shadow of a partial eclipse. At the Reformation David's shrine was completely destroyed, but leading Protestants eulogised the bishop for his doctrinal purity; free, they declared (quite disingenuously) of popish superstitions. His reputation was largely untouched by a campaign that was intended to remove the cult of saints from the history of Wales. Today it is the case, that beyond their localities, apart from David, the important Welsh saints are scarcely known.

The less legendary sources of early Welsh Christianity can be no less inimical to its founders. There is a widespread impression that archaeology simply offers evidence of their lack of literacy. An unfavourably damp climate has seen to the destruction of the earliest libraries; memorial stones are all that we have and their interpretation is a matter of contention: these inscriptions have been 'misread ... not by fools, but by the finest philologists, epigraphers, and historians, and patriots at that, with appalling consequences'. The perception of cultural standards in the emerging Welsh kingdoms is still formed on an assumption that because people at that time lived in primitive conditions they must therefore be lacking in intellectual achievements. The result has been 'inaccurate histories of the entire period'. Dr David Howlett (1998) ends his piece by saying of the 'Dark Ages', an oft used term, that it is a distinctly 'unhappy locution...... better not used'.

It is something of a paradox that the apparent mysteriousness of post-Roman Christianity is part of its appeal. Not much frequented, the sacred landscapes now offer a wonderful opportunity for quiet contemplation. In Wales, beauty, legend, art and architecture combine to give anyone who cares to visit the ancient churches and their holy wells many an hour of peaceful enlightenment. In Celtic parlance these are the 'thin' places, where centuries of prayer have gently eroded all division between earth and heaven.

ORDNANCE SURVEY SITE LOCATION REFERENCES

ANGLESEY

OS Landranger Map 114: Explorer Map 263:

Llanddwyn Island	387 627
Llangadwaladr Church	383 692
Seiriol's Well, Penmon	630 808

LLŶN PENINSULAR

OS Landranger Map 123; Explorer Maps 253 and 254

Clynnog Fawr Church	414 496
Llanaelhaearn Church	387 448
Cybi's Well, Llangybi	427 412
Llannor Church	354 372
Pistyll Church	328 423
Llangwnnadl Church	208 332
Uwchmynydd (Trwyn Maen Melyn)	140 252
Bardsey Island	120 215
Aberdaron Church	173 263

Local Tourist Information Offices supply free of charge, very clear maps of the coastal paths throughout Anglesey and the Llŷn peninsula.
(information available at time of publication)

Llangadwaldr Church, South Window

OPENING TIMES of CHURCHES

Chapter 1

The church ruins on Llanddwyn Island are always accessible except on the rare occasion of an unusually high tide.

Chapter 2

Llangadwaladr Church is open all year round from 10.30am to 4pm.

Chapter 3

Penmon Church is open all year round from 9am to 5pm. If taking a party of visitors, contact the rector on 01248 811 402.

Chapter 4

Clynnog Fawr Church is open from 11am to 4pm from the Saturday before Palm Sunday to school half term in October. For access to Llanaelhaearn Church contact the key holder on 01758 750 474, mobile 07787 953887, email: lynda.cox@llanaelhaearn.com, preferably at least a day in advance of your visit.

Chapter 5

Llangybi Church is usually locked during the week, but this does not affect access to Cybi's Well.

Chapter 6

Access to Llannor Church is by advance arrangement with the vicar on 01758 740 919.

Chapter 7

Pistyll and Llangwnnadl Churches are open all year round from dawn till dusk.

Chapter 8

Aberdaron Church is open from February to December, from 10am until 6pm or dusk, whichever is the earlier.

POST-ROMAN LATIN INSCRIBED STONES

Stones are listed in order of their present rather than that of any earlier location. Many have their origin in unexcavated sites beyond *llan* boundaries despite the fact that they may now be kept in the parish church. Bangor Cathedral Bookshop is able to provide up-to-date information about access to churches. Each translation of an inscription is followed by an estimation of its date, eg L5c - E6c = late fifth or early sixth century.

ANGLESEY

333 804 **BODEDERN** St Edern's Church. Inside north wall of the north side chapel.

ERCAGNI '(stone) of Ercagnos'　　　　L5c - 6c

383 692 **LLANGADWALADR** St Cadwaladr's Church – see chapter 2.

446 685 **LLANGAFFO** St Caffo's Church vestry, against the east wall.

(G)VIRNIN FILIVS CVVRIS CINI EREXIT HVNC LAPIDEM
'Guirnin, son of Cuuris Cini, erected this stone'　　　E7c

458 759 **LLANGEFNI** St Cyngar's Church porch.

CVLIDOR IACIT ET ORVVITE MVLIERI SECVNDI
'Culidor lies (here) and Orvvita his wife, (he was a son) of Secundus'
5c – E6c

(See also Ffynnon Gyngar under Sacred Wells)

553 758 **LLANSADWRN** St Sadwrn's Church, inside north chancel wall.

HIC BEA(TV)S ( ) SATVRNINVS SE(PVLTUS I)ACIT ET SVA
SA(NCTA) CONIVX PA(X VOBISCVM SIT)
'Here blessed ... Sadwrn (in the sepulchre) lies and his (saintly) wife.
Peace (be with you both)'

The Saturninus commemorated by this inscription has been identified with Sadwrn Farchog, founder of the church. Sadwrn may have been brother of St Illtud, who died between AD527 and AD537, which would give an approximate date for the monument of AD530.

356 745 **PENCARNISIOG** A4080 road, east side, protected by field boundary wall, between the village and A5 junction. Almost illegible:

CVNOGVSI HIC IACIT '(stone) of Cunogusus; here he lies' 5c – E6c
A name of Irish origin which gives the area its Welsh name Carnisiog.

480 859 **BRYNREFAIL**, Penrhoslligwy. Down the lane south, two thirds of a mile, St Mihangel's Church, inside chancel wall.

HIC IACIT MACCVDECCETI 'Here he lies: (stone) of Maccudeccetus' E6c

A mile to the south-west is Mynydd Bodafon, a natural amphitheatre of rocks around a beautiful glacial tarn.

BANGOR Gwynedd Museum (stone found at Capel Bronwen)
– translation by David Howlett and Charles Thomas:

(AVD)IVA SANCTISSIMA	'Audiva, a most holy
MVLIER HIC IACIT	woman, here lies;
QVE FVIT AMATISSI(MA)	who was the most beloved
CONIVX BIVATISI	wife of Bivatisus –
FAMVLVS DI SACERDOS	slave of God, bishop,
ET VASSO PAVLINI	and a servant of Paulinus.
AVDO COGNATIONE *ET*	From Audus by kinship,
OMNIVM CIVIVM	of all citizens'
ADQVAE PARENTVM EXEMPLA *ET*	and relatives' patterns
MORIBVS DISCIPLINA	in morals; in discipline;
AC SAPIENTIAE	and for wisdom –
AVRO ET LAPIDIBVS	than gold and precious stones
MELIOR (HEC) FVIT	this woman was better' 6c

(The conjunctions italicised show what appear to have been false corrections of the metre.)

91

BANGOR Gwynedd Museum (stone found on farmland at Llanbabo).

ETTORIGI H '(stone) of Ettorix (here he lies)   L5c – E6c

LLŶN PENINSULA

173 263 **ABERDARON** Church of St Hywyn & St Lleuddad – see chapter 8. Thomas (1998) suggests that the name Veracius on the first stone derives from Old Breton Uueroc, 'Amiable', an appropriate companion to Senacus, 'Venerable'.

482 455 **BRYNCIR** Llystyn Gwyn Farmyard.

ICORI FILIVS POTENTINI '(stone) of Icorix, son of Potentinus'   6c

Also in ancient Irish Ogam script 'Icorigas'.
Ogam letters were formed by scoring lines at angles across and to the side of a stone's edge; they are more commonly to be seen in Ireland and South Wales.

387 448 **LLANAELHAEARN** St Aelhaearn's Church and churchyard – see chapter 4.

ALIORTUS ELMETIACO HIC IACET
'Aliortus from Elmet lies here'   L5c- E6c

MELITV
'Melitus'   5c - 6c

329 314 **LLANBEDROG** Plas Glyn y Weddw Art Gallery – see chapter 6.

455 607 **LLANFAGLAN** St Baglan's Church (in the care of Friends of Friendless Chuches) inside, main door lintel.

FILI LOVERNII ANATEMORI 'a son of Lovernius, (stone) of Anatemor'

5c - 6c

(Ffynnon Faglan, marked on maps as if in a nearby field, has been filled in; a few carved stones from the well are in the nearby copse.)

295 289 **LLANGIAN** St Cian's Church burial ground, south side; weather-worn but still legible.

MELI MEDICI FILI MARTINI IACIT '(stone) of Melus, a healer, son of Martinus; he lies (here)'   5c - 6c

354 372 **LLANNOR** Holy Cross Church, entrance – see chapter 6.

540 417 **PENMORFA** Gesail Gyfarch Farm. Where the tracks divide, just before the farmhouse, take the one to the right for about 25 yards; there is a garden gate on the left. The stone can be seen on the other side, protected by a slate-topped shelter.

FILI CVNALIPI CVNACI IACIT BECCVRI '(stone) of Cunalipus' son, Cunacus; he lies (here) . . . of Beccurus'   6c

St Beuno's Church, Penmorfa (541 403) is in the care of Friends of Friendless Churches. It appears to be of post-Roman foundation, now 14c in nave. To find this building take a tight turn into the only lane that goes south-west from the centre of the village. There is excellent woodcarving to be seen and at the west end fragments of stained glass c1500, originally part of the east window, and in the porch some glass from the 1930s showing St Cybi with St Cyngar.

534 378 **TREFLYS** St Mihangel Church, against the north wall of the chancel.

IACONVS FILIVS MINI IACIT 'Jaconus, son of Minus lies (here)'

Preceeding this inscription is a rare British example of the Christian monogram promoted by the Emperor Constantine I after AD313. It was devised by intersecting *chi* and *rho*, the first two letters in Greek of the word 'christos' meaning 'the anointed one.'   6c

A complete list of post-Roman inscriptions in Gwynedd would require the inclusion of those not on Angelsey or the Llŷn peninsula. Among the most important of these are four stones on display in the disused church in Penmachno village, Snowdonia, one of which according to Thomas (1998) is encrypted. For more detailed information see *A Corpus of Early Medieval Insribed Stones and Stone Sculpture in Wales, Vol. III* (2013) by Nancy Edwards.

SACRED WELLS AND THEIR CHURCHES

The wells listed are among those of primary interest for the purposes of this book; for further information contact Cymdeithas Ffynhonnau Cymru, a voluntary organisation which holds lectures and conferences to assist local communities in the restoration and maintenance of these historic features.

ANGLESEY

349 840 FFYNNON AFRAN, **Llantrisant** (SE of Llanddeusant)
Now little more than a small pond near the lychgate of St Afran, St Ieuan & St Sannan's Church (in the care of Friends of Friendless Churches) down a lane just beyond Tŷ-mawr.

499 847 FFYNNON ALLGO, **Llanallgo**
This well is in Glanrafon Uchaf Caravan Park. A sandstone carved head discovered during excavation in 1982 suggests a pagan origin. Allgo was a brother of Gildas and not far from here is the *llan* to another brother, Eigrad, and a chapel to his sister Peithien at Lligwy. Less than a mile to the north can be seen the ruins of Din Lligwy (496 862) a settlement occupied around the second century.

386 628 FFYNNON DDWYNWEN, **Llanddwyn** – see chapter 1.

To the left of the path going west towards the ruins of the church is Ffynnon Dafaden (389 631) meaning 'Wart Well' – known for curing warts! It is now dried up, but the stone cavity with steps is still clearly visible. Also on the island is the spring Ffynnon y Sais (388 631) 'Well of the English', who were sustained here by its water whilst their boat was grounded.

465 933 FFYNNON EILIAN, **Llaneilian**

Take the passageway to the left of the entrance gate to St Eilian's churchyard (469 928). Pass through the farm gate, farmyard, kissing-gate, another farm gate and go down the fields toward the sea. Turning left onto the coastal path, continue in a north-westerly direction about 550 yards over the rock. There is a sudden descent into a *cwm* full of meadowsweet, orchids and rock plants. Just before a footbridge over the stream, the overgrown foundations of a well chamber can be seen to the left of the path, at the base of a little cliff. This water was reputed to cure fever, epilepsy and lymphatic disorders. Coins were thrown into the pool to bring a blessing on livestock and harvest. It was drained on occasion by the villagers and if found to contain fish or amphibians this was taken to be a bad omen. As befits Eilian who issued a curse (ch 5) slates bearing the initials of intended victims of bad luck have been found here, also, pennies slipped under the stonework to give effect to malevolent wishes. *Ffynhonnau* such as this, which flow to the north, could be used in this way: those which flow south only give effect to blessings.

The well's popularity up until the nineteenth century accounts for the still prosperous appearance of St Eilian's Church with its fine Norman tower and pyramidal spire similar to Penmon. Inside, the fifteenth century rood loft would on holy days have provided a platform for singers and musicians. On the roof corbels there are exquisite painted carvings of musicians playing flute and bagpipes. Above the screen's central arch, the blade of the grim reaper's scythe reads: *Colyn angau yw pechod*, 'Sin is the sting of death'. As at Clynnog Fawr, there is a passageway connecting the church to the saint's mortuary chapel. At one time two panels of this chapel's altar could be removed, allowing the sick to seek consolation by crawling into a curled position above the saint's grave. St Eilian's is open daily, May to September, 10am to 4pm.

423 737 FFYNNON GEINWEN, **Cerrigceinwen**

This healing well is in St Ceinwen's churchyard, on the left hand side of the descending path to the church main door. Ceinwen is reputed to have been a sister of Dwynwen.

457 758 FFYNNON GYNGAR, **Llangefni**

On the right hand side, a little way down the tarmac track leading to the dingle below St Cyngar's Church. Water trickles from the rock into a small pool protected by a wall. There is a post-Roman inscribed stone in the porch of the church.

(516 746) FFYNNON REDIFAEL, **Penmynydd**

Still marked on maps this well, sadly, has been lost to field enlargement. However, the church at the road junction is worth a visit; the hotel next door has a key. Gredifael was one of nine sons of the sixth century Breton and King of Usk, Dingad ap Nudd Hael. Like his brother Fflewyn, saint of Llanfflewyn, he was appointed leader of a *clas* in the monastery of Paulinus at Tŷ-Gwyn in Whitland (for Paulinus see Latin inscribed stone to Audiva in Bangor Museum). Another of Dingad's sons was Baglan, saint of Llanfaglan.

630 808 FFYNNON SEIRIOL, **Penmon** – see chapter 3.

259 754 FFYNNON WENFAEN, **Rhoscolyn Llanwenfaen**
Lanes to Rhoscolyn are lined with honeysuckle hedges. Just below St Gwenfaen's Church (268 757) there is an un-metalled road heading in the direction of a crow-step-gabled and turreted estate house. Walk along it, past the house and more modest dwellings and continue over the stile on to rough pasture land. Follow the ascent to the coastguard lookout, from which point take the path northwest about 450 yards. The well is just before the stile which gives access to Rhoscolyn Head.

Steps descend to an ante-chamber with corner seats; two small pools are separated by a rectangular wall, the first flanked by narrow seats, the second by steps. The water is reputed to cure unhappy mental states. Pebbles of white quartz known as charm stones would be cast into this well as an oblation to St Gwenfaen, their colour symbolic of the purity of her life, whose name means 'White Rock'. The view from here is spectacular and in keeping with the spurious legend that Gwenfaen scaled a coastal stack to escape the clutches of angry druids (the druids on Anglesey had in fact been wiped out by the Romans in AD60). As an incoming tide threatened to engulf the fugitive, she was carried off by angels.

LLŶN PENINSULA

384 446 FFYNNON AELHAEARN, Llanaelhaearn

A walk up the hill road running south-west from the top of the village. The well is on the left, on private land. The doors to it are kept locked now that it is used for a local water supply.

234 284 FFYNNON AELRHIW, Rhiw

Roads around Rhiw are single track but there is a small car park less than a mile from the well at the western end of Hell's Mouth, near the coastal path. Take the steep lane to the right, up past Plas yn Rhiw, and go to where the road curls around St Aelrhiw's churchyard. A few yards on from here, on the left along the lane which runs south-west toward the village look out for a double gate. Pass through it and go down to the right; the well is at the bottom of this *cae llefrith*, 'field of milk'. A gap at one end of an enclosure wall has steps which descend directly to the water, reputed to be effective for eye, skin and lymphatic disorders. The upright stone at the entrance seems to be a phallic complement to the femininity of the well. There is a ledge seat to sit on and the pool itself is surrounded by a pavement on all four sides. The view from here is awesome: Hell's Mouth, mountains of Snowdonia and Cardigan Bay. Ffynnon Saint is a mile to the north-east.

413 494 FFYNNON BEUNO, Clynnog Fawr – see chapter 4.

From a lane between the church and the well, crossing the by-pass, there is access to a Neolithic portal dolmen worth seeing, where the capstone is decorated with 110 'cup marks' – go toward the sea as far as Bach Wen Farm then turn left along the grassy lane for a distance of about 400 yards.

119 218 FFYNNON Y DALAR, **Bardsey**

This circular well cut and built into the rock at the top of *cae bryn baglau* can be seen just over the bank to the left of the island track, between Plas Bach and Carreg Fawr. It tends to run dry in summer.

403 486 FFYNNON DDIGWG, **Clynnog Fawr**

A large marshy hollow is all that accounts for this spring which arises in a culvert beneath the main road.

513 400 FFYNNON DDUNAWD, **Pentrefelin**

A spring runs from a field under the road and into the open field where drovers once rested their cattle. The well's structure remains, incorporated into the wall. Dunawd Fawr was a warrior-saint and son of St Pabo whose church (378 868) on Anglesey has a very fine *llan* boundary. Dunawd is credited with having founded a renowned Celtic monastery at Bangor Is-coed, just south of Chester. Here Gwynhoedl is said to have been trained. Early in the seventh century the monks at Bangor Is-coed were put to the sword by an army of Northumbrians led by King Aethelfrith.

274 367 FFYNNON DUDWEN, **Llandudwen**

In the south-east corner of the field, some 100 yards south of St Dudwen's, the only church to be consecrated to this female saint; like Dwynwen and Ceinwen she was a daughter of Brychan Brycheiniog. The water is said to cure eye disorders, fever, rheumatism, fits and muscular weakness. Secret weddings were contracted beside this well which lies out of sight of any nearby dwelling.

293 270 FFYNNON ENGAN, Llanengan

Walk down the track on the north side of St Engan's Church and continue around the right side of Tan-y-fynwent, having first sought permission of the householder to enter the rear garden. The healing well is about 50 yards beyond this house, a pool surrounded by a wall with stone seating on three sides. A little way downstream there is a pond, once used as a second pool for full immersion of the sick.

Llanengan Church is built over the grave of King Einion of Gwynedd, said to be 'golden-handed' for having given Penmon to his brother(?) Seiriol. Pilgrims could look west from here and see Bardsey Island as a spur to their final day's journey. Inside are fine Tudor screens carved with vines, little visages and some interesting creatures; on the choir stalls, there are stylised flora and mythical beasts. Like the sixteenth century antiquarian John Leland, one cannot fail to notice the offertory chest, Cyff Engan, with its three locks. No-one would dare pass this monster without making a resounding contribution in coinage, in imitation of pilgrims to the temple at Jerusalem (*St Mark* 12.41-44; *St Luke* 21.1-4). St Engan's is usually open on weekday afternoons throughout August.

139 252 FFYNNON FAIR (St Mary's Well) Uwchmynydd – see chapter 7.

226 314 FFYNNON FAIR, Bryncroes

A pilgrims' well at the crossroads near the chapel and the school. Enclosed by a narrow, stepped rectangular pavement and a low wall, this was a last stop before the final miles to Aberdaron.

309 308 FFYNNON FYW, **Mynytho Common**

A track to the right of Horeb Chapel leads down to this well, a sensitively restored walled enclosure around two pools reputed to cure eye disorders and rheumatism in the name of St Curig. The smaller pool is rectangular with steps on one side, the larger is square and surrounded by a pavement with steps at one corner. The view of St Tudwell's Islands and Cardigan Bay is without equal. Although the name Ffynnon Fyw translates as 'Living Well', it could possibly have derived from a pagan use of the word *dduw* when the water was looked upon as the eye of the 'god'. Access to the pool was at one time controlled by keepers who were notorious for embezzlement.

427 412 FFYNNON GYBI, **Llangybi** – see chapter 5.

Like Crochan Ddwynwen, Cybi's Well was also used for love divination. A young woman would cast her handkerchief onto the surface of the water; if it floated south the object of her affections was faithful, if it drifted to the north he was not to be trusted.

219 328 FFYNNON LLEUDDAD, **Llangwnnadl**

Off the B4417 as it approaches from the east the lane which leads down to the church. What was once a track forming part of a public path runs south from Carrog Farm to an area of land that is a mire full of aquatic flora. The well is about 50 yards south along the western boundary, obscured by undergrowth.

242 294 FFYNNON SAINT, **Rhiw**

If approaching by road from Rhiw village continue down past the entrance to Plas yn Rhiw for half a mile to where there is a diagonal crossroad. The coastal path and car park at the western end of Porth Neigwl (Hell's Mouth) are just out of sight to the right; the way to the well is in the opposite direction, along the track to Ty'n-y-parc. Continue past the house (up on the left) and into the wood. About a quarter of a mile beyond the forestry shed there are three huge eucalyptus to the left; the track almost doubles back on itself as it ascends to a field gate onto the mountain. To the left is a short flight of shallow stone steps and a path which passes through a walkers' gate, beyond which lies the well. Boulders surround a pool on four sides with steps either side of the top end. This water is fast flowing and is good for eye infections. A mile to the south-west, higher on Rhiw mountain and in the open fields is Ffynnon Aelrhiw.

Remains of St Dwynwen's Church

CONSERVATION

It is not easily seen, that miniscule circle on an OS Explorer map which marks the site of a well. The joy of discovery can be short-lived if on going to the site there is nothing to be found. At Penmynydd in Anglesey and Llanfaglan in Arfon subsidised land improvement sealed their fate: public paths linked the holy wells to their associated churches, no longer in use but saved nonetheless; the wells were destroyed to make the fields more efficient. In another example, a saint's well in Eifionydd was demolished for a car port; the nearby church was preserved by a charity.

For more than thirty years Reverend Eirlys Gruffydd and her husband, Ken, have been amassing information about the holy wells of Wales (cf Bibliography). Their research has won respect from the owners of *ffynhonnau* and local authorities. Four sacred wells have been restored in Llŷn ; the latest, Ffynnon Dudwen, reopened and reconsecrated by the Bishop of Bangor. Oversight of such projects is with the help of a body known as Cymdeithas Ffynhonnau Cymru. In the south of Wales and across the Welsh borders Wellsprings fulfils a similar function.

The upkeep of country churches is always a matter of local concern. Where there is no caretaker, nearby parishioners may have devised a rota for opening the building during the hours of daylight. If there is no longer a worshipping congregation and the site is unsuitable for an alternative use, a fifty-year-old charity, Friends of Friendless Churches, may accept the building as a gift. With ownership transferred, the fabric is renovated and the interior re-opened. Of the forty churches which the FFC owns, ten are in Gwynedd and Anglesey; the diocese pays for 30% of the maintenance while the rest is made up with funds from the state. The parishioners continue with day-to-day management: key-holding, cleaning and care of the burial ground.

BIBLIOGRAPHY

BARING-GOULD, Sabine & FISHER, John, *The Lives of The British Saints*, 4 volumes, Honorable Society of Cymmordorion, London, 1907-13.

BARTRUM, Peter C, *A Welsh Classical Dictionary, People in History and Legend up to AD1000*, National Library of Wales, Aberystwyth, 1993.

BORD, Janet, *Cures and Curses: Ritual and Cult at Holy Wells*, Heart of Albion Press, Market Harborough, 2006.

BOWEN, EG, *The Settlements of the Celtic Saints in Wales*, University of Wales Press, Cardiff, 1956.
Saints, Seaways and Settlements in the Celtic Lands, University of Wales Press, Cardiff, 1969.

BROWN, Peter, *The Cult of the Saints, Its rise and function in Latin Christianity*, SCM Press, London, 1981.

CHITTY, Mary, *The Monks on Ynys Enlli*, AD500-1252, Aberdaron, 1992.

DAVIES, Oliver, *Celtic Christianity in Early Medieval Wales*, University of Wales Press, Cardiff 1996.

DAVIES, Wendy, *Wales in the Early Middle Ages*, Leicester University Press, 1982.
Patterns of Power in Early Wales, Clarendon Press, London, 1990.

DOBLE, GH, *Lives of the Welsh Saints*, University of Wales Press, Cardiff, 1993.

EDWARDS, Nancy, & LANE, Alan, *The Early Church in Wales and the West*, Oxbow, Oxford, 1992.

EDWARDS, Nancy (ed), *The Archaeology of the Early Medieval Celtic Churches*, Maney Publishing, Leeds, 2009.

GRUFFYDD, Eirlys & Ken Lloyd, *Ffynhonnau Cymru, cyfrol 2*, Gwasg Carreg Gwalch, Llanrwst, 1999.

HASLAM, Richard, ORBACH, Julian and VOELCKER, Adam, *The Buildings of Wales, Gwynedd*, (Pevsner Guide), Yale University Press, New Haven & London, 2009.

HENKEN, Elissa R, *Traditions of the Welsh Saints*, DS Brewer, Cambridge, 1987.

HOWLETT, David R, *Cambro-Latin Compositions, their Competence and Craftsmanship*, Four Courts Press, Dublin, 1998.

JONES, Francis, *The Holy Wells of Wales*, University of Wales Press, Cardiff, 1954.

LYNCH, Frances, *Gwynedd*, Her Majesty's Stationery Office, London, 1995.

MILLER, Molly, *The Saints of Gwynedd*, Boydell Press, Woodbridge, 1979.

NASH-WILLIAMS, VE, *The Early Christian Monuments of Wales*, University of Wales Press, Cardiff, 1950.

PETTS, David, *The Early Medieval Church in Wales*, History Press, Stroud, 2009.

PRITCHARD, TW, *St. Winefride, Her Holy Well and the Jesuit Mission, c.650-1930*, Bridge Books, Wrexham, 2009.

ROGERS, Byron, *The Man Who Went Into the West: The Life of RS Thomas*, Aurum, London, 2006.

ROWLAND, Jenny, *Early Welsh Saga Poetry: A Study and Edition of the Englynion*, DS Brewer, Cambridge, 1990.

THOMAS, Charles, *Celtic Britain*, Thames & Hudson, London, 1986.
Christian Celts; Messages and Images, Tempus, Stroud, 1998.
Whispering Reeds, or the Anglesey Catamanus Stone Stript Bare, Oxbow, Oxford, 2002.

WADE-EVANS, AW, *Vitae Sanctorum Britanniae et Genealogiae*, University of Wales Press, Cardiff, 1944.

WARREN, FE, *The Liturgy and Ritual of the Celtic Church*, (1881), with introduction by Jane Stevenson, Boydell & Brewer, Woodbridge, 1987.

WINTERBOTTOM, M, *Gildas: The Ruin of Britain and Other Works*, Phillimore, Chichester, 1978.

TEA SHOPS

Places for refreshment near the main sites:

Ch 1. Marram Grass Café, 2/3 of a mile south of Newborough, near roundabout where A4080 makes a 100 degree turn – open most of the year.

Ch 2. Llys Llewelyn Tea-rooms, Aberffraw – seasonal.

Ch 3. Cottage Café and Garden, Penmon Point – seasonal.

Chs 4-6. Caffi'r Tydden, Tyddyn Sachau Nurseries, Y Ffôr – all year round.

Ch 7. Mair Fish's Beach Café, The Old Fishermans Store, Whistling Sands, Porth Oer – seasonal.

Ch 8. Cegin Fawr, Aberdaron – seasonal

Caffi'r Oriel, Plas Glyn y Weddw, Llanbedrog – all year round except Tuesdays in school term time.

Graham Murphy studied Theology at Manchester University and trained near Ruthin to be a professional gardener. His book *Founders of the National Trust* appeared in several editions, including a Japanese translation. He has also published in the NT Garden Series, contributing the volumes on *Wildflowers* and *Old Roses*.

Eve Goldsmith is a fine artist, a graduate of St Martin's School of Art.

Drafts of the text were read for compositional advice by the designer Candida Boyes.